From Silence to Sanctuary

A guide to understanding,
preventing and
responding to abuse

JANE CHEVOUS

First published in Great Britain in 2004 by
Society for Promoting Christian Knowledge
Holy Trinity Church
Marylebone Road
London NW1 4DU

Scripture quotations are taken from the HOLY BIBLE, NEW
INTERNATIONAL VERSION Inclusive Language Edition, copyright © 1995
by International Bible Society. Used by permission of Hodder & Stoughton Ltd,
a member of the Hodder Headline Plc Group.

British Library Cataloguing-in-Publication Data
A catalogue record for this book is available from the British Library

ISBN 0–281–05639–0

1 3 5 7 9 10 8 6 4 2

Designed and typeset by Kenneth Burnley, Wirral, Cheshire
Printed in Malta by Gutenberg Press Ltd

Contents

————◄○►————

Acknowledgements

————◄◊►————

This book would not have been possible without the support and assistance of many people. In particular, I am indebted to a number of survivors who have courageously shared a part of their journey and their reflections to contribute to this book. Your stories and insights are the heart of the book to me and the revelation that will illuminate and inspire people to action. I am deeply grateful for the opportunity to use them here. Whether it felt safe for you to be named or not, you know who you are. Thank you.

I dedicate this book to the following people:

To my birth-mother for the start of life

My adoptive family for my growing

My Creator for new life

Jon for being the cherished arrow from my bow

Ivan my angel for unconditional and joyous love

Kate for steadfastness, wisdom and true friendship

Karen my enlightened witness and model princess

Concetta for sisterhood

Sue for being my mentor-writer

The Chevous clan for extended family

And to all the many who have shared their stories and musings, all whose lives have touched mine on the journey: thank you for the rare privilege.

Introduction:
from despair to hope

———◄○►———

Getting the act together

In 2002 Churches Together in Britain and Ireland (CTBI) commissioned and published an excellent report on sexual abuse: *Time for Action: Sexual abuse, the Churches and a new dawn for survivors*. Archbishop Rowan Williams described it as 'sometimes devastating reading, but timely, necessary and – if we are prepared to hear and act on some unwelcome truths – ultimately hopeful'. Last summer a panel consisting of some members of the working group who wrote the report, and survivors of abuse contacted through the Survivors' programme featured at the Greenbelt festival,[1] debated what progress the report had instigated. It became clear that while there were some encouraging signs, there was not the passion, urgency or thorough grasp of the issues that the survivors hoped for. Yet this is an excellent report and I could not imagine a better fuel to fire the energy and engagement of the churches on this issue. So why have the flames not burned?

The previous summer I had been among the informal group of survivors who organized that Survivors' programme at Greenbelt, and I spoke at two of the seminars, about the issues of abuse and how Christians could approach prevention and response. This led to an article in *Third Way* magazine, 'Breaking the Silence', in which I argued the case for open recognition and more justice in our response.[2] There were no letters in reaction to the article and of a number of friends and colleagues who saw it, only three ever made any comment. I don't overrate my skills as a writer, but my advisers judged it a reasonable piece. Normally *Third Way* articles promote a healthy debate. Why had I failed to break the silence?

In some ways I struggle to answer these two questions. Both the book and my article, along with many others I've read by other competent and powerful writers, were well researched and challenging. Both gave practical suggestions as to what could be done to understand and respond better to what has been, and prevent what might be. Both were courageous, painful, moving and compassionate, practical, theological and comprehensive. The programme at Greenbelt was a great example of grass-roots action, organized not by any constituted organization but a group of individuals with a passion for justice who had been given a platform. What more do we as caring individuals and organizations need?

A new approach?

I wrestled with this question for most of last year and came up with three tentative conclusions:

1 The subject is so painful to hear, such a hot iron to perhaps our deepest wound, that we need to hear it many times before we can respond in any functional way and at other than a deeply personal level.

2 Existing books and articles tend to focus on only one aspect of abuse and are more often read by survivors and their families or professionals after an incident has powerfully affected their lives. Bombarded by issues and tasks competing for our attention and bewildered by the range and choice of resources available, there is still a need, in the European context at least, for a short, practical and hopefully easily digestible resource that aids the transition from shame, guilt and disgust to positive action.

3 Many existing publications focus more on the problem and less on the solution. This has been understood as necessary because people like myself, already informed and passionate about the issue, so often come up against apparent denial and ignorance that we assume education and information to be the key. But what if the education itself is such a distressing and depressing process that willing readers feel abused themselves by the impact of what they are learning? Instead of leading out, the process of education becomes one of closing down. It can also risk reinforcing stereotypes: like my half-African son once said to me, 'How can I feel good about being a black African when the images I see on the TV are all of rural-dwellers living in poverty, disease and famine, none of which connects at all with my life or presents me with a positive model?' If the realities of abuse stun us into inactivity, maybe it is time for a different approach focused on positive activity and hope.

The 'triumph of hope over experience'

One of the important ideas to grasp is that a survivor hears silence as indifference. Silence from others also gives more space for the abusers' voices to repeat their destructive false messages. Breaking the silence involves more than just speaking out. It requires a corresponding refrain from those who have heard; a move forward that signals comprehension, absorption and ownership. It is with this refrain in mind that I have approached this book. The book is written from my value-base and identity as a Christian and includes some attempts at theological reflection, because if I can't make sense of this theologically, the value of my faith is challenged. It is written with particular advice to those working in the Church or in Christian organizations such as care homes or youth projects, where there is a need for good practice based on Christian principles. There are two particular reasons for this: the observation that Christian institutions have a poor track record in this area, and the significant number of survivors who report ignorant, unhelpful and even abusive responses from Christians and churches. However, I hope the principles, if not the theology, are still interesting to others concerned about abuse and that the suggestions for developing practice are applicable in most contexts. I hope, too, that any individual who desires a better world, a safer community, a supportive relationship, will find here insight and guidance for their own part in making it so.

Living beyond

There has been something of a debate among people who have experienced abuse about appropriate terminology. There is a sense of progression for many people from being a (powerless) victim, to survivor, to (recovered) thriver. At different times, 'victim' can feel too negative and 'survivor/thriver' too positive. Some books choose to avoid such terms altogether for that reason, adopting a neutral approach, such as 'people who have been abused'.

I have deliberately chosen to stay with the term survivor; initially because I find it acknowledges the huge impact abuse has on one's life and identity but recognizes a progression from victim state. Then a colleague led me to the etymology of the word, which goes beyond the usual sense of endurance or continued existence. Its earliest origins seem related to the Sanskrit *jiv* meaning victuals, then the Latin *supervivere* and French *survivre* both meaning to live over, above, close to or beyond. The richness and movement of these shades of meaning struck me. Here is a word that hints at the journey from being trapped by the abuse, to overcoming its legacy and moving beyond into new life; from the passivity of victim to the value of provider. I have not just out-lived;

I have lived beyond. In the beyond I am outside of the limits placed by the abuser, and the resurrection echoes in that image hint at the taste of paradise God spreads out as a feast to enjoy in that place.

Using this book

The first two chapters sketch out the experience of abuse of power in our society and the effects on those whose lives it touches. Chapter 3 suggests some principles to underpin our response to abuse and efforts to improve prevention. The following five chapters address how to respond to situations of abuse, including supporting survivors and working with people who have abused; and offer guidelines for adopting practice to prevent abuse developing. Chapter 9 explores significant theological themes from a survivor's perspective. At the end of each chapter are some discussion questions, and at the end of the book is a collection of recommended resources. There are six appendices:

- Appendices 1 and 2 provide guidance and information for anyone involved in discovering and reporting child abuse.
- Appendices 3 and 4 are for church and community leaders responsible for developing good practice in child and adult protection and reporting of abuse.
- Appendix 5 offers positive strategies for survivors.
- Appendix 6 gives advice to families, friends, professionals and anyone supporting survivors of abuse.

Notes

1 Greenbelt is an annual Christian Arts Festival that includes a programme of seminars and workshops on a variety of topical world issues and theological perspectives.
2 The article was published in the January/February 2003 issue (Vol. 26, No. 1).

1

The Spoilt Garden:
understanding abuse, its prevalence,
causes and collusions

———◀○▶———

'Beauty for Ashes'

When you walk through the valley
Of the shadow of death
When you walk through this garden of tears
Even in the darkness
My hand will lead I will comfort you
Beauty for ashes, joy instead of mourning
Beauty for ashes, hope for despair
Hope will rise again

If you knew how I loved you
With an unchanging love
How I long to return you to grace
In Me is your freedom
I am your peace
Turn again to the rock of your past
Beauty for ashes, joy instead of mourning
Beauty for ashes, hope for despair
Hope will rise again

If you stretch out your hand
To the poor and oppressed
Only then will your light rise again
I am your greatness
I your true might
This land will be lost without Me
In this time of uncertainty
Of tumult and change
When you're lost in a sea of despair
I feel all your sadness I feel your pain

I've walked sorrows road
But from death I can bring you new life
Beauty for ashes, joy instead of mourning
Beauty for ashes, hope for despair
Hope will rise again

I will bend down and heal you
I will gather you up
As a mother the children she loves
If you make Me your desire
If you walk in My ways
If you humble yourselves to My cause
Beauty for ashes, joy instead of mourning
Beauty for ashes, hope for despair
Hope will rise again.

copyright © Charity Quin, singer-songwriter.
www.charityquin.com tgbtg[1]

When Christians grieve or protest about war, about debt and poverty, about prejudice . . . about the abuse of children or the neglect of the helpless elderly, it is because of the fear we rightly feel when insult and violence blot out the divine image in our human relations, the reflection to one another of the promise of Jesus in one another. (Archbishop Rowan Williams, enthronement ceremony, 2003)

The song 'Beauty for Ashes' was written in response to the events of September 11th, 2001, events that both embodied and grew out of poverty, war and abuse – some of the fundamental evils of our world. The song speaks of the incredible promise that God will restore the divine image, even where we have blotted it out so successfully. As the Archbishop suggests, these are more than simple flaws or small in-adequacies; these are outrageous atrocities that wound the earth, spread subversively throughout the fabric of society like a malignant canker and are tenacious in character, voracious in appetite and pernicious in effect. We already know a lot about them and are exposed to further condensed scenes each day through the media. But this is not enough to remove the problems or reduce their effects. Understanding and knowledge are empty vessels without application and engagement. So this is an offering of a tool for positive action on abuse. It speaks from the wisdom of those who have experience of abuse but brings the triumph of hope that moves beyond despair and apathy. This perspective suggests we need to move from the isolation of silence towards the sanctuary of loving community.

There is a spectrum of ways to abuse, from open physical coercion to secret sexual domination, from verbal bullying to charismatic manipulation, and including spiritual and emotional humiliation and control. The most manipulative, hidden abuse is often the hardest to identify, as behaviour and interactions may appear perfectly healthy. This book brings them together not just because they are all about abuse of power but also because there is a shared dynamic of control, common patterns of behaviour and similar experiences of the consequences for victims and the surrounding community. I have drawn from different examples of abuse of power within families and institutions, bringing together the insights that emerge to identify integrated solutions. The survivors network I belong to has made the deliberate decision to include all types of abuse as we find so many of the issues and patterns of experiences are the same, and our inclusiveness brings empowerment and shared learning.

I have listened to a young black man describe his experience of growing up in Zimbabwe and a young white woman from England describe her experience of incest. The words they used to describe the effects of in the first case an oppressive society and in the second case an oppressive family were almost identical. A sense of worthlessness and powerlessness dominated both their childhoods, and the response – to work harder than ever to prove they were as good as other people – was almost identical in each case. The emotions emerging from their story – of despair, anger and hope – were echoes of each other.

I have used a number of examples to illustrate the experience, dynamics and consequences of abuse and responses by individuals and institutions affected by it. Each brings its particular gifts of insights to the discussion. A consideration of domestic violence helps to understand the nature of offending behaviour. Abuse of children has four specific categories (described below), which provide tighter parameters to the definition. Abuse of power, friendship and intimacy in relationships is a key issue for those in ministry and leadership and focuses training for prevention. Emotional abuse has consistently appeared as a significant phenomenon in cults and fundamentalist religious groups and contributes to an audit of cultures that promote abuse. Echoes from an even wider shared experience of oppression (for example, racism and sexism) bring new insights and strategies. As this is designed to be a practical rather than scholarly resource, I have not attempted to represent a balanced overview of the types of abuse and their prevalence.[2] Rather the aim is to provide an accurate experience of abuse: the reality of the flaws, the strength of their effects, the camouflage that makes detection and elimination difficult.

What is abuse?

Abuse is a powerful phenomenon involving extreme emotions and experiences. In training leaders in child protection and abuse awareness and good practice, at most training sessions we begin by creating a word-wall of whatever we first associate with the term 'abuse' (see Figure 1). The results are always powerful and disturbing.

---

exploit   take advantage of   misuse   manipulate   maltreat   neglect

molest   insult   mistreat   batter   hurt   harm   injure   cruelty   violence

invective   misconduct   sin   destructive   pain   hunger   anger   control

fear   rejection   overpower   secrecy   loneliness   shame   guilt   stress

depression   suicide   torture   self-harm   prostitution   mind-control   kill

destroy   diminish   defend   victimize   humiliate   isolate   threat   rape

batter   imprison   exclude   harass   expose   burn   beat   break

obsession   possessive   undermine   unpredictable   shout   scream

swear   lock up   fear   murder   urinate   forced sex   blame   intimidate

destroy   normalize   minimize   assault   pornography   neglect

emotional abuse   spit   extreme temperatures   starve   animal abuse

punish   bullying   paedophilia   worthless   victim   accusation   silence

---

Figure 1   Word-wall

This book is concerned with abuse in relation to the exercise of power in a variety of contexts within our local communities, including families and institutions. The common core is an abusive act or relationship, which may be defined as one causing unnecessary or unwarranted harm to another person, either intentionally or unintentionally, within the structural power dynamic of a leadership or authority relationship; or through force resulting from greater strength, social conditioning or substance abuse, e.g. the 'date rape' drug (Ormerod, 1995, pp. xi–xii, adapted). In effect, the core of an abusive act is the violation of another person's boundaries and this demonstrates the importance of abuse being defined by the victim; not all of us draw our boundaries in the same place, and the level of abuse will be experienced differently by each of us. Some areas are outside the scope of a book of this length: organized ritual or sadistic abuse is a contentious and specialist field; the abuse of those in ministry and their families by the congregation or community they minister to is related but deserves separate consideration;[3] abuse on a national scale, by oppressive leaders such as Saddam Hussein or Robert Mugabe, is beyond my knowledge base. I have concentrated more on abuse within a defined relationship because (a) this is the case with the majority of abuse, and (b) physical or sexual assault by strangers brings in a different field of, for example, football-match or nightclub violence, particularly among young men, which as a dynamic has clear differences from the main types of abuse being considered and would distort the analysis and conclusions too much.

Common examples of abuse that we currently recognize include:

- child abuse
- sexual or physical abuse by siblings, partners, professionals
- rape or assault by strangers or 'dates'
- emotional or spiritual abuse or manipulation by leaders or families

In relation to the Christian community, the book has a particular focus on the three areas of abuse most likely to take place within the church context. First, child abuse, which may take place within the life of the church itself or may be brought in through the lives of individual members who may be child victims, adults abused as children, abusers and the families and close neighbours of all these people. Second, pastoral abuse, in particular manipulation, bullying, emotional abuse and/or sexual misconduct by clergy and pastoral leaders. Third, spiritual abuse, which includes the use of spiritual authority to control or dominate another person and may impose a controlling spirituality on the victim (Johnson and VanVonderen, 1991, pp. 20–3).

Child abuse

Child abuse definitions provide an appropriate starting point that also reflects the change in our understanding of and attitude to abuse over the last 40 years. We began to be aware of 'battered baby syndrome' in the 1960s, as a result of publications from the USA. Professional concern over non-accidental injury was heightened after the enquiry into the death of Maria Colwell in 1974. Public awareness followed during the 1980s as a result of a number of high-profile reports into child deaths. Professional concern over sexual abuse also intensified during this period, coming to public attention with the Cleveland inquiry in 1988. This prompted a new debate about the ethics and effectiveness of intervention into family life. The resultant learning focused on protecting the safety and welfare of the child and resulted in new principles being laid out in the Children's Act of 1989 and the Working Together document of 1999. New learning is still emerging from the Climbié and Huntley cases and this will undoubtedly bring fresh perspectives on practice over the next few years.

The statutory bodies currently record abuse of children within four categories, as defined below (Department of Health et al., 1999).

General definition: abuse and neglect

Somebody may abuse or neglect a child by inflicting harm, or by failing to act to prevent harm. Children may be abused in a family or in an institutional or community setting, by those known to them or, more rarely, by a stranger.

Neglect

Neglect is the persistent failure to meet a child's basic physical and/or psychological needs, likely to result in the serious impairment of the child's health or development. It may involve a parent or carer failing to provide adequate food, shelter and clothing, failing to protect a child from physical harm or danger, or the failure to ensure access to appropriate medical care or treatment. It may also include neglect of, or unresponsiveness to, a child's basic emotional needs.

Physical abuse

Physical abuse may involve hitting, shaking, throwing, poisoning, burning or scalding, drowning, suffocating, or otherwise causing physical harm to a child. Physical harm may also be caused when a parent or carer feigns the symptoms of, or deliberately causes ill health to a child whom they are looking after. [*There is currently some controversy about the diagnosis of this latter syndrome.*]

Sexual abuse

Sexual abuse involves forcing or enticing a child or young person to take part in sexual activities, whether or not the child is aware of what is happening. The activities may involve physical contact, including penetrative (e.g. rape or buggery) or non-penetrative acts. They may include non-contact activities, such as involving children in looking at, or in the production of, pornographic material or watching sexual activities, or encouraging children to behave in sexually inappropriate ways.

Emotional abuse

Emotional abuse is the persistent emotional ill-treatment of a child such as to cause severe and persistent adverse effects on the child's emotional development. It may involve conveying to children that they are worthless or unloved, inadequate, or valued only insofar as they meet the needs of another person. It may feature age or developmentally inappropriate expectations being imposed on children. It may involve causing children frequently to feel frightened or in danger, or the exploitation or corruption of children.

I suggest these definitions can also be applied to the abuse of an adult by another adult who has power and influence over them, either within a leadership relationship, family relationship or through intimidation or coercion.

Prevalence of child abuse

The culture of silence that has surrounded all manifestations of abuse, and the culture of secrecy cultivated by abusers create a real difficulty in identifying accurately how many people have been abused and how many are being abused. There is a reliance on a number of different indicators to paint an impressionist picture of overall prevalence and still some significant gaps in the areas of research. The indicators are themselves quite clear and support the common conclusion from those in the field and those whose lives are caught up in abuse, that it is both under-reported and widely experienced.

Key indicators
The child protection register
This is a register of children who have been identified by Social Services and the key agencies responsible for child protection as having been abused and/or at risk of abuse.[4] This does not provide an overall rate of abuse – (answering the question 'how many children have been abused?') – but records how many children have been identified by the statutory agencies as being at continuing risk of significant harm, at any one time. The latest published statistics are for the year 2000. On a given date there were 30,300 children and young people on the register. By adding children who pass through the system, either coming off or going onto the register during the year, we get a truer figure of over 55,000 children who were on the register at some point during the year. Of those on the register, the percentages registered under the different categories (see definitions given above) were as illustrated in Figure 2.

Neglect	44%
Physical Abuse	33%
Sexual Abuse	17%
Emotional Abuse	15%

More girls (21%) than boys (14%) were registered for sexual abuse.
More boys (34%) than girls (33%) were registered for physical abuse.
Some were put under more than one category.

Figure 2   Child Protection Registrations

We know from other indicators, including cumulative counting, the number of children reporting to independent organizations such as Childline or the National Society for the Prevention of Cruelty to Children (NSPCC) and the evidence of abusers and adults reporting historic abuse, that the actual number is higher than these statistics indicate. The NSPCC, for example, quotes recent research as revealing that 1 in 10 of young people have suffered serious abuse or neglect during childhood. Each week at least one child will die as the result of an adult's abuse. A quarter of all rape victims are children.

Children in need

'Children in need' is the term used to describe those children and young people who are known to their local Social Services department as requiring the provision of services. Figure 3 shows the situation as at February 2000.

Abuse can be seen as the single most important cause of the need for intervention into family care. It represents a significant cost to society – over £1 billion a year is spent on services investigating and responding to child abuse.

400,000 children in need.

64,000 of those were 'looked after' (in foster or residential homes).

80,600 were due to abuse or neglect.

= 35% of total children in need, 56% of those looked after.

12% were disabled children.

16% were from ethnic minorities (1.5 times % of total population).

Figure 3   Children in need

Crime statistics and offender profiling

The most useful major review of research into abusers I have found looks specifically at those who have committed sexual offences against children. However, the trend of the conclusions within this review is repeated in the available information relating to other areas of abuse, so it is possible to interpolate some common themes.

First, it is widely accepted that official statistics relating to abuse significantly underestimate its prevalence and the nature of the offence. The main reasons for this are:

- under-reporting
- charges withdrawn due to a reluctance from the victim to proceed, or to insufficient evidence
- plea-bargaining or lack of evidence leads to lesser charges

These factors are identified in research relating to the underestimate of the rates of sexual offences, domestic violence and abuse of power by those in leadership.

In the case of sexual offences against children, the majority of these offences (80 per cent) take place in either the victim's or the offender's home – the abuser knows the victim. Only about one third of offenders would fit the label 'paedophile' that is used to describe people with a significant deviant sexual attraction to children. The majority of offenders (60–70 per cent) target only girls; about 10 per cent are not specific about gender. There is evidence of networks of offenders, with four main forms:

- within institutions such as residential care homes
- within extended families
- groups of paedophiles who share material over the Internet or share victims
- a single offender with a ring of victims (often using one victim to recruit others)

The picture of child-abuse rings can be blurred with child prostitution and pornography. The scale of this problem is really unknown; it is estimated that over 5,000 British children (under 16) are involved in prostitution (*Childhood Matters*, 1996). However, most offenders work alone and associate rather than act with other abusers to share information and gain moral support.

Another difficulty in gaining an accurate picture relates to the way offences are recorded. National published statistics do not always make the age of the victim clear (depending on the chosen charge) and regional statistics recorded by individual forces include some variations in the data collected and are not centrally collated and analysed. Some trends that are demonstrated are:

- children are more likely to be victims of rape and indecent assault (including buggery) than adults of the same gender
- age 10–15 is the most vulnerable for becoming a victim of these offences (Grubin, 1998)
- the link between domestic violence and both physical and sexual child abuse is clear; in possibly as high as 60 per cent of cases, men known to be violent to their partners were also abusing the children (Humphreys, 2000)

- There is also now a recognized link with the abuse of family pets, and the Royal Society for the Prevention of Cruelty to Animals (RSPCA) is working with child protection agencies as a front-line agency in child protection.

Domestic violence is used to group together a variety of abuses of power within the home; not just physical but also verbal, sexual, emotional and spiritual abuse. It is perpetrated by both men and women against both men and women; however, both evidence and research clearly indicates a higher incidence of abuse by men towards women. Abuse also takes place within the home by children to siblings, where this is what they have learnt to do from adults around them.

Most studies suggest that 1 in 4 adult women will experience domestic violence at some point in their lives. Domestic violence accounts for 1 in 4 of the violent incidents reported to the British Crime Survey and an incidence of domestic violence takes place in the UK every 6–20 seconds, with someone being injured approximately every 10 seconds.

- Men are far less likely to be subjected to a repeated pattern of abuse and are less likely to report being hurt, frightened or upset by what has happened.
- Nearly 1 in 5 men admit to having used violence against their partner or ex-partner at least once; only 37 per cent claim they would never act violently.
- There are children aged 16 or under in half of the households affected by domestic violence.[5]

Some other types of abuse are either not recognized as crimes (for example abuse of trust within pastoral ministry) or are so unlikely to be reported as a crime or reach criminal proceedings that official statistics are not a useful indicator (for example, sexual misconduct with an adult hinges on the issue of consent, which is hard to prove; emotional abuse within a marriage is hard to identify as breaking any law). So the testimony of survivors of both current and historic abuse becomes crucial evidence in establishing the scale of the problem.

Survivors' experience

We know that by its very nature abuse is secretive and difficult both to report and to prove. Therefore, research has looked to population surveys and survivors reporting in order to gain a more accurate picture of the true extent of cases of abuse. There are a number of different significant research sources both in the UK and the USA that suggest that 1 in 4 girls and 1 in 9 boys experience abuse in childhood.[6] This is widely accepted by the agencies involved in dealing with abuse to be a more realistic indicator than the number of known children at risk or the number of reports or convictions.

One of the issues that makes a significant difference to the number of adults who report having been abused is the way the question is framed. Survivors can minimize what has happened to them through a reluctance to use common labels to describe their experience. For example, a survey asking adult women about sexual assault found they were less likely to report they had been raped and more likely to agree that someone had forced them to have sex without their consent. Other factors affecting reported prevalence include methodology (e.g. surveys, interviews) and participation rates. So, widely differing rates are found; for example in surveys in 21 countries, from 7 to 36 per cent of women and from 3 to 29 per cent of men reported they had been sexually abused as children (Finkelhor, 1994). One of the best UK studies (Baker and Duncan, 1985) found 12 per cent of women and 8 per cent of men reported they had been sexually abused before the age of 16 (including non-contact abuse such as exposure to pornographic material and 'flashing'). The victims knew about half of the abusers and women were more likely than men to be abused at a younger age (10 and 12 respectively).

Consistent trends in the various surveys include:

- the rates for abuse of girls is higher than boys
- girls are more likely to be abused within the family
- girls are more likely to report being abused by men (90 per cent of reported abuse)
- reports by men abused as boys have wider variations in the gender of the abuser
- about a half of all victims state they never reported the abuse

Grubin (1998, p. 12) points out that it is difficult to explain the widely disparate estimates one gets of the number of children who are abused each year in England and Wales – varying from 3,500 to 72,600. What is interesting, he says, is that the highest figure comes from the police crime reports (not victim surveys); he suggests further scrutiny of these to gain a sharper picture.

Prevalence of other areas of abuse

When it comes to the prevalence of other types of abuse of power, I have been unable to discover an authoritative, comprehensively researched answer. By its very nature, abuse of power is extremely hard to detect or disclose. Certain cases come to the public attention: doctors abusing patients, or care workers abusing elderly people in residential homes. In the context of religious communities, we know about the big cases that hit the headlines; Chris Brain and the Nine O'Clock Service (NOS),

David Koresh and Waco, Jim Jones and Jonestown. The rise in popularity of the discipling and shepherding movements have seen an
environment emerge that appears to be a ready breeding-ground for
abusive control. Chrnalogar (2000, p. 20) defines an abusive group as
one that 'exerts coercive persuasion through systematic deception'.
Mainstream denominations are not immune to the temptations of
abusive leadership. Research in the USA found that 20 per cent of
ministers and priests had sexually abused one or more members of their
congregation (Beasley-Murray, 1998, pp. 69–70). Indeed it has been
pointed out that 'there is even some evidence that in conservative
Christian homes where there is an ethos of discipline, obedience to
authority and rigid codes of moral behaviour, the likelihood of abuse is
actually greater' (Gosney, 2002, p. 4).

A UK study demonstrated that abuse of power is an equally serious
and widespread phenomenon here. In a survey of 141 practising
ministers, 21 per cent admitted to having succumbed to the temptation
to sexually inappropriate behaviour with someone else. Clearly this is a
comparable figure with the US survey. In the same survey, 57 per cent
said they had often imposed a worship style; only 8 per cent thought
they had never manipulated meetings; 85 per cent had forced a course
of action, if rarely (Beasley-Murray, 1998, pp. 69 and 86). Margaret
Kennedy, who heads MACSAS, a support and advocacy group for
people abused by clergy or ministers,[7] did not need to try hard, when
working on a research project, to discover over 70 women abused by
clergy as adults. But further research is clearly needed, especially in the
UK, which is significantly behind the USA in this area.

We are increasingly recognizing cases of spiritual abuse, and one of
the significant issues here is the double effect on our spiritual life. The
abuser has the additional authority of divine power behind him; and the
victim often has their faith or spiritual identity damaged or even
destroyed because of the nature of the abuse. One of the saddest aspects
of the Christian survivors' networks I have experienced is the number
of people who have been spiritually abused, often on top of other
abusive experiences, by the very community they looked to for support
and a life-giving spirit. The examples of good and bad practice are at
best evenly matched. I am convinced we can and must do better than
this. Where pastoral and spiritual abuses are concerned, the results of
the Climbié Inquiry mean it is not only church members who will be
interested in the findings.

Causes of abuse

It is important to recognize there is no simple answer to the question,
why do people abuse other people? Within a complex picture that has
many layers and shades, there are some recognizable trends and signifi-

cant factors. There is no universal agreement about these, so I highlight here some of the latest thinking and in particular the issues that make most sense of the survivors' experience.

It's a male problem

The majority of known sex offenders are men, and more adult victims of sexual abuse and other violent and sexual crimes, such as rape and domestic violence, are female. Most church leaders are men. There is an obvious argument that power abuse is a gender issue: '[sexual] violation of trust is an epidemic, mainstream problem that re-enacts in the professional relationship a wider cultural power-imbalance between men and women' (Rutter, 1995, p. 2). The research on the proportion of women committing sex offences against children, for example, demonstrates that although population surveys indicate a slightly higher figure than the 3.5 per cent of allegations recorded, it is not likely to be more than 15 per cent of all offences (Grubin, 1998). There is also evidence that a number of women are coerced into offending by their male partner.

It is important that acknowledging abuse as a 'male problem' is not used to further silence male victims, particularly those abused by women (which is more likely to be boys than girls). Some of the issues concerning this are highlighted later in this chapter.

Clearly a recognizable gender difference is there in the pattern of human behaviour, but like the observation that violent parents have violent children, debate rages about whether this is inherited (genetic pre-disposition to violence), causal (learnt behaviour), or a reaction to external factors. So blame may be placed on pathology, culture, gender, stress, the victim's personality or behaviour, the environment or social construction. In the Church, the fundamentalist mindset and the dangers of power have been identified as key factors.

It stems from social construction

Influential thinking from the field of domestic violence argues that 'the socialization of men encourages an ideology that teaches and affirms violence by men to women; further, the society we live in is made up of sexist social institutions, dominated by men, which support men's power and control over women, and our history traditions and myths condone and support men's oppression of women' (McMaster and Swain, 1989, p. 70). A tolerance of attitudes that condone abuse or at least give permission for it to continue must share some responsibility; for example, research has shown that 1 in 5 young men and 1 in 10 young women think that abuse or violence against women is acceptable (Burton et al., 1998).

Studies of those who commit sexual offences do indicate a link with childhood experiences, with about one third indicating they developed their sexual interest in children during adolescence. It is harder to substantiate claims that perpetrators of abuse are unassertive and socially deficient, except in that minority of offenders who target boys outside of the family. Perpetrators do report loneliness and a lack of intimacy, suggesting that they turn to children to meet a need they are unable to sustain in adult relationships. This all suggests that greater studies in the development of healthy emotional and sexual attachments in adolescence would be helpful in identifying potential abusers and developing successful preventative techniques.

It's confirmed by abusive theology

We see the fruits of institutional sexism in both theology and practice; in 'might is right' theology. For example, some people interpret the creation and fall events in Genesis 2 and 3 as promoting male domination as the true order of life, in contrast to the suggested equality of Genesis 1.27: 'in the image of God he created them, male and female he created them'. Some Christians take certain of St Paul's teachings as universal principles; for example, submissive wives in Ephesians 5.22–24 and the headship of men (1 Corinthians 11.3). Yet other conventions they recognize as cultural – seen many women with shaved heads recently (1 Corinthians 11.6)? So they ignore the implied reciprocity in interpersonal relationships – husbands to wives (Ephesians 5.25–30), parents to children (Ephesians 6.1–4,) masters to slaves (Ephesians 6.5–9) and our equality in God's eyes: 'In the Lord, however, woman is not independent of man, nor is man independent of woman. For as woman came from man, so also is man born of woman. But everything comes from God' (1 Corinthians 11.11–12). A dualistic and dogmatic position within any of the main streams of Christian thought can lead to different examples of abusive beliefs. Evangelicals may defend the inerrancy of Scripture in order to keep wives submissive and men in headship. Charismatics may maintain the power of the Spirit is proof of God even when it is used to dominate and coerce followers into dubious practices. Catholics may use Mariology as an image of flawless virginity, to oppress women's sexuality. This theological critique is developed into an alternative theology in Chapter 9.

It's original sin

There is a theological argument that the abuse of power is the paradigm consequence of original sin. Humans are not equipped to deal with their separation from God, and the awareness of power that stems from the Fall is perhaps the most significant legacy of the act of gaining knowledge. It is an argument of incompetence; we are attempting to deal with things we don't understand. This echoes Bonhoeffer's observation that stupidity, rather than evil, is our greatest danger: 'any violent display of power, whether political or religious, produces an outburst of folly in a large part of mankind; indeed . . . the power of some needs the folly of the others (Bonhoeffer, 1971, p. 8).

It's cyclical behaviour

Work with abusers highlights a pattern of offending behaviour that is repeated, often escalating in severity of abuse. There is a differentiation between habitual offenders, who abuse many victims and may display predatory behaviour, and those (the majority) who offend within a particular context, usually their family. There can be a link with the abuser's own family experience which may indicate learnt or adapted behaviour; but research on sexual offenders, for example, has shown that while a higher than average proportion of offenders report they were abused, 'a history of sexual abuse as a child is neither necessary nor sufficient to lead to adult sexual offending' (Grubin, 1998, p. vi).

Suggested links include:

- Learnt behaviour, i.e. copying what has been witnessed/experienced.
- Displaced aggression (which echoes research with children and young people who bully), i.e. anger and frustration of abuse taken out on a weaker victim.
- Normalization, i.e. coping with abusive behaviour by accepting it as normal, unharmful and therefore permissible to repeat with others.
- Acting out, which may happen unconsciously, during 'flashbacks'[8] or as a way of processing the feelings generated by the abuse.
- Adapted behaviour due to stunted growth or because of the coping strategies adopted at the time, e.g. later problems in attachment and sustaining positive adult relationships.

However, while all of these possibilities fit both the observations of professionals and researchers and the experiences of some survivors themselves, there is such a range and variation of responses it has not been possible to identify a conclusive and universal pattern. There are many more examples where survivors have progressed to enjoy happy, healthy and successful lives – or just the normal mixture of peaks and troughs! So a history of abuse is inadequate as a complete explanation of what creates an abuser. Perhaps the truth is that combinations of the various factors contribute to different abuse scenarios. In Chapter 6, I consider the application of some of these ideas in working with people who have abused.

Collusions

It is not just an individual with a predisposition to abuse that creates an abusive situation. There are many environmental, social and organizational factors that can cause, aggravate or collude with the abuse.

Identifying key factors that feed the abuse points to the good practices we need to adopt in order to starve it out.

Families at risk

Abuse is no respecter of class, race, or status. It is taking place in all types of families in all types of contexts. However there are some risk factors that can increase the likelihood of abuse, or make it easier for an abuser to function. These include the obvious effects of social exclusion, poverty and disadvantage, which increase stress and reduce the family resources to deal with major problems such as abuse. Chronic health problems and mental health issues, including those associated with drug and alcohol abuse, are also common contributory factors. We have already identified how one type of abuse can lead into another, for example domestic violence leading to child and sexual abuse and cruelty to animals. Poor relationships between parents and children are strongly associated with child abuse (although may provide opportunity more than cause). Sibling abuse is still in the early days of research, but appears to have a higher incidence in families where other abuse is already taking place. The short answer is that abuse is more likely to take place in a family that is severely under stress and that develops an abusive culture, whether in order to deal with the stress or as a result of previous experiences.

Abusive organizations

Brubaker (quoted in Plante, 1999, pp. 135–71) identified that abusive organizations have a profile similar to that of the most abusive families. I have adapted and expanded his profile to summarize key characteristics:

- Social isolation and a closed system, i.e. self-sufficiency and outside relationships are discouraged or forbidden.
- Blurred boundaries and a lack of individuation, i.e. roles and personal/professional or adult/child boundaries are distorted; individual autonomy is discouraged and group identity imposed.
- Shame-based perfectionism: impossible demands are made and humiliation is used to isolate and control those who inevitably fail to meet expectations.
- Distorted communication or 'no talk rule': information may be deliberately sabotaged, communication both within and outside blocked or forbidden.
- Unequal power or authoritarianism: oppressive dictatorship rather than democratic.
- Fundamentalism: a presentation of inerrant truth that leaves no room for question or disagreement and must be strictly adhered to.
- Dependency: a culture that demands reliance and ultimately enslavement.

- Exotic experience: unusual, exciting or bizarre practices, which may be attractive and seductively counter-cultural but eventually abusive and dysfunctional.

A similar set of characteristics can be used to identify cults, but is not unknown within new religious movements including apparently Christian communities. The Nine O'Clock Service (NOS) in Sheffield is a documented recent example – see Howard (1996) for a researched documentary. Concerns about similar abusive dynamics have been raised about some other newer expressions of Christian community, including the extremes of the Charismatic and heavy shepherding movements and fundamentalist groups in the USA particularly. (See Chapter 10 for some publications in this area.) In the chapters on good practice, I explore alternative models of community and leadership that could prevent such abusive powers from developing.

Abusive leadership

The more extreme, cult-like groups are often formed around a few or even one significant, dominant and abusive individual. It would be a mistake to think that 'ordinary' families, groups and churches are therefore immune to such dangers. There is a clear consensus about some of the risk factors that can produce abusive leadership even within mainstream culture (see e.g. Beasley-Murray, 1998; also *Time for Action* Report 2002.) These include:

- fuzzy boundaries
- unclear role
- stressful role and/or home life
- isolation
- lack of supervision and support
- collusive organizational culture
- vulnerable 'clients'

If we recognize abusive leadership and culture against a scale rather than a static definition, then we can identify potentially worrying movements towards the more extreme examples of these aspects in many groups, and adjust our practice before an abusive situation develops.

Vulnerable victims

Abuse is not the victim's fault in the sense that they are the least powerful in the relationship, but it is worth recognizing that certain groups of people are particularly vulnerable to abuse, and trying to understand why that is the case. Often it is simply about being an easier target and both less able to defend themselves and having less access to escape or disclosure. These groups include:

- children, especially those in care
- women and girls
- the elderly
- people suffering mental distress
- disabled people
- people from ethnic minorities
- people who have been previously abused

The significance of the last category should not be missed. It is not uncommon for survivors to report multiple experiences of abuse, including the worst imaginable scenarios of disclosing the abuse to a counsellor or minister, only to be re-abused by the very person turned to for help. Again I am emphatically not suggesting that the victim is to blame for their abuse. I do recognize, though, that having been a victim once, I may develop (often unconscious) behaviours that increase my vulnerability and can even feed the abusive behaviour of authority figures. Learning to identify and change these, to protect myself at a reasonable level, is one of the transforming steps of healing. This can complement the initiatives responsible communities need to take in order to protect the most vulnerable among us.

Collusive cultures

Even aware and well-meaning communities can unknowingly collude with the perpetuation of abuse. It happens when we avoid talking about the issues and maintain the silence that has characterized abuse. It happens when we are naive about the reality and think 'it can't happen here'. It happens when we avoid confronting bad practice because we are afraid for ourselves, for reputations or of hurting others. We collude when we ignore the issue, minimize it, or dismiss survivors or whistle-blowers as irrational, vindictive or exaggerating. It is not surprising that we do all these things; it is a difficult, uncomfortable and distressing subject. It is important that we try to recognize when we are colluding and aim to avoid continuing to do so.

Tricky issues

In recent years our increased understanding of abuse has led to more effective strategies for prevention and response. The progress made overall serves to highlight key areas that need further research and development. I mention three current issues that I believe merit particular attention: male victims and female offenders; adolescent sex offending; and the smacking of children.

Male victims and female offenders

It is important to recognize that for male survivors who have been abused by women, it can be even harder to disclose the abuse, because of our stereotypical images of abusers and of men as strong role models. As one such survivor explains:

> I know that there are many, many men out there who have like me suffered at the hands of their Mothers. Who like I did are struggling with what has been done to them and the effect this is having on their lives. They are finding it difficult because:
> 1 They feel that they are alone that whenever they hear of abuse cases it is mostly Men against Women or Children not Mums against Sons.
> 2 It is not the thing to do to be seen to be weak in this culture of ours. The Man needs to be seen to be strong in all that they do.[9]

Outside of institutional abuse, it has clearly been harder for men to report being abused, particularly if an abuser was female. The difficulty is becoming increasingly recognized, but there is still a significant task to be done to give boys and men the same permission to report abuse, of whatever type, and to have their voices heard.

A study of female sex offenders raises some interesting issues. One immediate difficulty is defining what is abusive behaviour by women; as Grubin (1998, p. 23) points out, even though emotionally unprepared for overt sexualized behaviour, 'the child may be encouraged to view the event as proof of his virility'. As with all other forms of abuse, the unconditioned perceptions of the victim and the harmful effects should be the defining criteria for what is appropriate. A mother has no more rights than any other carer to invade the privacy of a child's body, especially for her own pleasure.

Population surveys indicate that women abuse boys more than girls, yet research with female offenders and child victims evidences no particular gender bias. Grubin (1998) suggests this is because the larger number of women (over half is estimated) abuse with a male partner. Many women state that their partner coerced them into committing the abuse, although they may continue to abuse on their own. Adolescents are more likely than adult offenders to act alone, and possibly use more force. Babysitters form a significant group (about one fifth of offences), and the majority (60 per cent) happen within the family.

This suggests several courses of action are needed. While it would not be justified to significantly divert resources from dealing with male offenders, there is still an educational and advocacy job to be done with and for boys and men, in the context of raising awareness within society as a whole. The evidence from victims that the tenacious 'macho' image creates silence, along with the obvious links with violent offences, suggests a lot more needs to be done to provide positive, assertive and cooperative models for men and women. The Christian community has a particular responsibility here. While Jesus was no pushover, he clearly rejected violence and abuse of power by the (male) hierarchy of his day. Churches that promote the headship of men over women need to be careful they are not reinforcing a male stereotype of unemotional domination, and a female role of submission. This provides too many opportunities for both women and men to abuse and be silenced.

Adolescent sex offending

It is significant to note that about 30 per cent of all sex crime is committed by adolescent sex offenders. A proportion of this would be defined as 'age appropriate' activity (i.e. peer sex) and therefore not an indicator of serious sexual deviancy – only a small minority go on to commit sexual offences as adults. However, the fact that many adult perpetrators reported that it was in their adolescence that their deviant sexual interest began, means it is important to develop the ability to identify this high-risk category early on.

One of the difficulties here is that we don't have enough information about normal adolescent sexual behaviour to be able to successfully identify and predict deviancy. Research and government agendas (in, for example, the fields of health and youth work) have been more concerned with particular consequences than sexual activity itself. So, although there is good information and resources about sexual health, contraception and teenage pregnancy, there is less solid research about the current prevalence of teenage sexual activity – although what there is makes interesting reading. The majority of young people report their first sexual experience at age 13 or 14; their first sexual intercourse at 16; and the main reasons for first intercourse as being in love and curiosity. Peer or partner pressure is a significant factor for a minority. The younger they were at first intercourse, the more likely to later regret it: 20 per cent of males and 42 per cent females aged 16–24 felt it had been too soon. There is also a gap in our understanding of how adolescent sexual experience translates into what we might identify as 'normal' adult sexual behaviour. A further difficulty is obvious here, in that there is no societal consensus about what is 'normal' within the wide boundaries of what is legal. It becomes a moral judgement, and faith groups are much more willing than governments to pronounce on such matters. Perhaps it is fear of the moral and ethical dilemmas that has created the reluctance to interfere in teenage sexual experimentation.

Certainly in 30 years of youth work, I have experienced an ineffective approach in both faith-based and secular policy and implementation. Christian groups have generally been clear about promoting their particular teaching: usually affirming committed, loving relationships and sexual intercourse within marriage as the normative standard. However, this doesn't face robustly the choices that most teenagers are making.

The maintained youth service has changed over the last three decades, as different governments have adopted new priorities; what has not changed significantly is the emphasis on young people making informed decisions about their own lives. Current government policy on sex and relationships education (SRE) is informed by a critique of the US system of abstinence education. 'Just Say No!' campaigns are largely perceived as ineffective in both drugs and sex education. In response, a comprehensive SRE programme is recommended that emphasizes sexual health, the importance of protected sex, and assisting young people's decision-making, judgements and behaviour. The only moral framework given is the importance of marriage and stable relationships and the ability to make independent and responsible decisions. The test of such a broad objective is in the curriculum detail. The emphasis is on harm prevention; contraception and safer sex feature strongly, abstinence is not mentioned (DfEE, 2000). Most concerning is the implicit message that is communicated – that it is normal and accepted that a significant minority of teenagers will have full sexual intercourse before the legal age of consent. For example, a government website for teenagers states '*only* about one in four young people under the age of sixteen have sex' (my italics).[10]

There is an opportunity here for Christian educators, families and communities to develop a balanced 'third way' in relationships. Simple abstinence messages clearly do not take enough account of young people's views and experiences and the influence of modern culture and youth subculture on their beliefs and choices. We all need to be equipped for the reality of the world we are in, or a dangerous duality develops; I have seen this in some church youth groups, where within the Christian community, traditional values are embraced with apparent enthusiasm, but behaviour once out 'in the real world' accommodates to the norm for their peer group. Some churches react to this by promoting closed friendship groups and strict same-faith partnerships and marriage; but this can lead to the kind of ghettoization and dependency that is linked with potentially abusive situations.

A healthy approach should deal with the reality of pressures and choices that young people face, and adopt the good practice of promoting responsible decision-making. Equally it should be developed within a clear value framework that gives equal attention to stability, abstinence and celibacy as it does to choice, experimentation and diversity. An important part of the maturation process is recognizing and learning to deal with the grey in moral issues, as well as learning to draw and sustain moral boundaries.

Smacking

There is currently a certain tension in the debate about whether it is ever justified to hit or smack children as part of disciplining them. There is an obvious generational divide: up until the 1960s, there was little questioning of the use of corporal punishment in the home and the school as a way of correcting children's 'bad' behaviour and teaching them correct behaviour. Today we are in a different world, with a much greater understanding of human development and in a legal context where, in many other European countries, there is no protection of a plea of 'reasonable chastisement' – if a parent hits a child, it is as much an assault as if the victim were an adult.

There is a school of thought in Christian circles that has legitimized physical punishment as appropriate correction, its acceptability reinforced by connecting it with the idea that Christian homes are counter-cultural, upholding positive moral values through good discipline. I believe this is an erroneous but dangerously seductive connection that provides a way of legitimizing violence. I can see no rational basis for believing that children need less protection from violence than adults, and that it is all right for the very people who are supposed to be taking care of them to be allowed to abuse them. Physical assault is physical abuse in any context, and is never acceptable.

I maintain that children learn several things from being smacked that go against what we desire them to learn, particularly that there is legitimacy in bullying and hitting. Of course, it is important that children have boundaries and learn how to behave ethically and considerately. There are other more successful techniques of positive discipline that enable this, modelling good behaviour and teaching children appropriate control and influence over choices and decisions. It will happen at times that we don't achieve this ideal; none of us is a perfect parent. However, I think the God who challenged the exclusion of children from his presence and presented them as a model for the kingdom, wants all children to grow up without the threat of violence.[11]

The challenge of preventing abuse of children and teenagers is central to the aim of developing relationships where abuse is less likely to occur. If we can raise our children within an environment that retains something of the innocence and safety of Eden, we create the foundations for healthier communities for generations to come. Recognizing and tackling the reality of abuse and its consequences becomes a starting point for new life.

Notes

1 Lyrics of the song 'Beauty for Ashes' by Charity Quin, quoted with permission. Based on verses from Isaiah.
2 Different kinds of abuse provide different illustrations. For example, danger is best illustrated through physical abuse, which is more likely to lead to fatalities; long-lasting effects through sexual abuse, which is recognized as causing particularly devastating trauma and stress for many years.
3 However, this can be a contributory factor and will be considered briefly in Chapter 7.

DISCUSSION QUESTIONS

To discuss

The research indicates that between 1 in 4 and 1 in 10 people experience abuse. This suggests that we all know someone who has been abused, if we haven't been ourselves. What is your experience of abuse? How do you feel about some of the facts quoted in this chapter? Was there anything that surprised you, or that you disagree with?

To reflect

I have suggested that the Church has both contributed to and colluded with abuse, through abusive theology and misuse of power. How do you understand God to exercise power? What place do violence and domination have in God's Kingdom? What gospel message speaks most strongly to the reality of abuse in our world?

To do

One or more of the three tricky issues highlighted could provide a focus for action on abuse.

1 What could you do to encourage male victims to gain a voice and support for healing? What support is already available in your community?

2 You could use materials from the NSPCC or the Children are Unbeatable Alliance (see Chapter 10) to debate and possibly support a campaign against the corporal punishment of children. Eleven other European countries have already made it illegal; should the UK be next?

3 How do you feel about the fact that 1 in 4 young people have sex before the age of 16? Should we have a more urgent and high-profile debate about this issue? What can you do to help young people to develop healthy and moral relationships? How can you support those who work with them, e.g. youth workers, teachers, parents?

4 Normally after an investigation and assessment that may involve social workers, police officers, health workers, teachers and others with key knowledge of the child(ren) concerned.

5 Statistics taken from the Domestic Violence Data Source, <http://www.domesticviolencedata.org>

6 For example, see the website of the Rape Crisis Federation Wales and England 2001, <http://www.rapecrisis.co.uk/support1.htm>; see also Baker and Duncan (1995), pp. 45–67, and Brooker et al. (2001), pp. 249–89.

7 Minister and Clergy Sexual Abuse Survivors (MACSAS) is contactable at PO Box 46933, London E8 1XA. An sae is appreciated.

8 A flashback is like a re-experiencing of the original abuse, often triggered by a particular event or sensual experience (e.g. a smell, taste, touch). It can include the visual (like a slide-show), physical (e.g. pain) and emotional (e.g. terror, desolation) realities of the abuse.

9 Quote from a survivor, DR 2002, used with permission.

10 <http://www.lifebytes.gov.uk/sex/sex_choices.html>
11 See resources section in Chapter 10 for information about the NSPCC
and the Children are Unbeatable Alliance.

References

Baker, A. W. and Duncan, S. P., 'Child sexual abuse: A study of prevalence in Great Britain', *Child Abuse and Neglect* 9, 1985, pp. 457–67.
Beasley-Murray, P., *Power for God's Sake, Power and Abuse in the Local Church*, Paternoster Press, Carlisle, 1998.
Bonhoeffer, D., *Letters and Papers from Prison* (enlarged edn), SCM Press, London, 1971.
Brooker, S., Cawson, P., Kelly, G. and Wattam, C., 'The Prevalence of Child Abuse and Neglect: a survey of young people', *International Journal of Market Research*, Vol. 43, No. 3, 2001.
Burton, S., Kitzinger, J., Kelly, L. and Regan, L., *Young People's Attitudes Towards Violence, Sex and Relationships: A survey and focus group study*, Zero Tolerance Charitable Trust, Glasgow and Manchester City Councils and Fife Council, Scotland, 1998.
Childhood Matters: Report of the National Commission of Inquiry into the Prevention of Child Abuse, HMSO, London, 1996.
Chrnalogar, M. A., *Twisted Scriptures: breaking free from churches that abuse*. Zondervan, Grand Rapids, 2000.
Department for Education and Employment (DfEE), *Sex and Relationship Education Guidance*, DfEE, Nottingham, 2000.
Department of Health, Home Office and Department for Education and Employment, *Working Together to Safeguard Children*, HMSO, 1999.
Finkelhor, D., 'The international epidemiology of child sexual abuse', *Child Abuse and Neglect* 18, 1994, pp. 409–17.
Gosney, J., *Surviving Child Sexual Abuse: Supporting Adults in the Church*, Grove Books, Cambridge, 2002.
Grubin, D., *Sex Offending Against Children: Understanding the Risk*, Policing and Reducing Crime Unit, London, 1998.
Howard, R., *The Rise and Fall of the Nine O'Clock Service: A cult within the church?* Mowbray, London, 1996.
Humphreys, C., *Child Protection and Woman Protection: Links and Schisms. An Overview of the Research.* Women's Aid website, <http://www.womensaid.org.uk/campaigns&research/research/child%20protection.htm>, accessed 19 February 2004.
Johnson, D. and VanVonderen, J., *The Subtle Power of Spiritual Abuse*, Bethany House Publishers, Minneapolis, 1991.
McMaster, K. and Swain, P., *A Private Affair? Stopping Men's Violence to Women*, CP Books, Wellington, 1998.
Ormerod, N. and T., *When Ministers Sin: Sexual Abuse in the Churches*, Millennium Books, Alexandria (Aus.), 1995.
Plante, T. (ed.), *Bless me Father For I Have Sinned: Perspectives on Sexual Abuse Committed by Roman Catholic Priests*, Praeger, Westport, CT, 1999.
Rutter, Peter, *Sex in the Forbidden Zone; When men in power abuse women's trust*, Aquarian, London, 1995.
Time for Action: Sexual abuse, the Churches and a new dawn for survivors, The Report to Churches Together in Britain and Ireland of the Group established to examine issues of Sexual Abuse, Churches Together in Britain and Ireland, London, 2002.

2

Daily Crucifixions: effects on victims, families and communities

◄◦►

Jesus hears the thump of a maul on metal: once, twice. He feels a spike probing the bones in his right arm: once, twice, three times. As the bones separate and the spike bites the hard wood, a dull pain pulses up into his armpit and his neck. This is the will of the Father . . .
    Jesus wants to howl his grief to the black skies. He cannot touch his mother anymore. He cannot receive her love anymore. Oh, God! – in his condition he is not worthy of the love of anyone. And this! Is the will . . . of the Father!

Wangerin, 1996, pp. 805, 807

Abuse can be like an experience of daily crucifixion. There is an element of deliberate torture in all abuse. The victim may represent a scapegoat for the family or institution within which the abuse is taking place. The consequences for the survivor and all touched by abuse entail further brutal sacrifices. This may disturb as an image and appear far-fetched, but the physical, emotional and spiritual suffering that a victim of abuse experiences is not easily imagined or understood by others. The crucifixion is a powerful message that Christ accepted and shared a similar fate, suffered in a similar context, and speaks loudly to survivors of abuse as to slaves, victims of war, torture and other oppressions.
    Certainly the effects of abuse on its victims are recognized as coming within the same framework as those of other major traumas, being both profound and long lasting. Of course each person's experience, both during and after the abuse, is as infinitely varied as the people and situations involved. There are, however, significant experiences and common issues, which give us some insight into the reality for many survivors. This understanding is key to framing an appropriate and adequate response.

Isolation

The grooming process that often begins the cycle of abuse isolates the targeted victim from the family and wider community. It is common for victims to believe they are the only one, to discover later that siblings or other members of the same group were being abused at the same time. The abuse is often prefaced by the positive affirmation that you are chosen or special – lifting you into a category apart from your peers. Within the family context, the abuser may take steps to keep public contact to a minimum, discouraging close friendships and visitors, to maintain control and ensure victims don't realize that other families do not behave like this. A manipulative manager will run a team on a divide-and-rule basis, feeding off our natural competitiveness, insecurity and tendency to protect our position.

The isolation of abuse is often perceived as sustaining a hidden, secret activity. Actually I don't believe this is completely true. I believe the signs of abuse are often obvious; we just can't or won't always recognize or interpret them correctly (see Chapter 4). It is true that the majority of abuse is likely to happen without witnesses, but not always. Some can be daringly public – an apparently innocent game, bouncing a child on a lap, provides an opportunity to touch her between her legs even within a room full of people. Friendly remarks – 'we'll have a good time together later, won't we?' – can hide threats and humiliations. Or the abuse can be daringly public but others hesitate to intervene because of fear of involvement and potential repercussions.

The betrayal of trust that is the fundamental flaw of the abusive relationship causes a profound reaction with the victim. Here is my parent, mentor, partner, whom I admire, trust, love and respect; here is my youth worker, mission leader, priest, manager, who many others also respect and trust. They are good people who have my interests at heart. So if the way they treat me leaves me feeling bad or unhappy, it must be something wrong with me.

Silence

The result is the victim is effectively silenced. 'Don't tell' is the ultimate imperative. There are many reasons why this command is obeyed: because you don't know what to tell; because you think this is normal; because you are told no one will believe you, it's all your fault, you will be punished, others will be punished because of you, you will cause the break-up of the family/organization . . .

Fear and shame are effective secret-keepers. These can be compounded by a deep sense of being somehow responsible for what happened. An abuser will cross a boundary slowly and with calculation – it can begin with a touch on the hand or a hug; an invitation to a drink after work; a request to help with a special task. Because you have already said 'yes' to the first step, it can be much harder to say 'no' to the next and the next, and this is used as evidence that you 'asked for it'. So the misconception that your own badness led these things to happen is reinforced, and the whisper of your voice is cut off.

Some groups of survivors may face particular struggles to have their voices heard. As previously highlighted, men are one group who we find it especially hard to listen to:

> The Church, the one place that they expect to feel safe and the place where they expect to find understanding, does not in fact understand. They are told in sermons and in person when they try to broach the subject that they should forgive and forget (this I am glad to say has not been my experience).
>
> Society does not understand. It has been both mine and others experience, that when they do try to get things sorted, i.e. through counselling, that quite often the reaction is one of disbelief. We are told that this does not happen and that we are imagining the things that happened to us. This only has the effect of propping up the feelings of being alone and having no hope.
>
> I am in a place where I can dispel some of these from my own experience. But there are many men out there who need to know that there is hope for them.[1]

The call to listen forms one of the foundational messages of this book; whether to children trying to signal their living nightmare, or to adults relating abuses of power by other adults, or historical abuse. The need to tell, to have your experience validated, to begin to hope that change is possible, eventually becomes overpowering and survivors dare to speak. This first 'little voice' is easily missed or crushed and communities could help by learning to listen more intently, with a gentle acceptance of the teller and an open mind and heart.

Destruction

I don't believe in a hierarchy of abuse – all abuse is potentially destructive and the first incident can have as traumatic an effect as the last. There is evidence that the strength of the effect can vary according to the individual personalities, upbringing and how firm are the foundations on which the abusive relationship is built. Some victims don't survive; they are murdered by their abuser or take their own lives, either directly or as a result of self-destructive interventions such as drug or alcohol misuse. Others experience healing apparently easily, have few long-term effects and seem able and content to put it all behind them. Most survivors whom I meet or read about struggle for years, on a long and difficult journey to a new life that can never fully restore what has been lost and damaged (although many people experience an element of substitution with different, better things: a transformation).

Research in the area of domestic violence illustrates this effectively. Key factors affecting the impact of the abuse include the nature of the relationship within which the abuse occurs, and the likelihood that it has occurred repeatedly over a period of time. The result is that more people are badly affected by domestic violence than other types of violent crime, the affects are greater, last longer (especially the psychological effects) and may include a significant alteration in lifestyle (Kershaw et al., 2000).

Self-worthlessness

There is an overall picture of destruction: confidence in oneself and what should be a secure environment is stolen; if I cannot trust my mother, who *is* trustworthy? If I cannot stop my body from physically responding to what is done to it, how can I trust myself? Here is the ultimate recipe for self-worthlessness; you are nothing, a bad person, who causes bad things to happen and who deserves them. Survivors struggle to makes sense of the incomprehensible with a tortuous logic that anyone outside the situation could soon break down.

Everything conspires to maintain survivors in that lowest position. The abuser will have given clear and hidden messages that I am worth less than nothing; that is why I am being treated in this way. In an attempt to make some sense of the situation, and still predisposed to think well of my abusers (especially if our relationship means I hold them in love and esteem), I judge and condemn myself. It cannot be their fault so it must be mine. I didn't stop them. I didn't leave. I kept going back. They are right – I asked for it/deserved it. These distorted messages are reinforced by some of our popular myths; husbands have a right to discipline their wives and children; females in sexy clothes are provoking men and asking for it. If at least part of my consciousness can acknowledge my innocence, this may only serve to underline my worthlessness. I am then faced with the stark reality of the world's injustice, the unanswerable 'why did it happen to me?' and the understandable perception that God didn't choose to save me – there was no miracle here.

Impurity

Shame is the most paralysing aspects of (sexual) abuse. The shame of the abuser is most often carried by and in the shame of the abused. This is because it is very rare for an abuser to own their own guilt and therefore carry the responsibility for their actions. The shame is then internalised into the victim and they begin to live out of that. Standing with someone and helping them lay the blame at the right person's door helps to ease the paralysing effects of shame. (Mitchell, 2003)

Whether sexual, physical or emotional, all abuse can leave the victim feeling ashamed and violated. The feeling of being unclean and being perceived as impure comes from within but may also be reinforced by other people's reactions. Ignorance or prejudice can lead to others suggesting that somehow the victim asked for the abuse or at least colluded with it, heard as meaning that it was deserved. In some churches, the lack of judgement, so clearly modelled by Jesus, is a significant counterpoint that enables a survivor to gradually shed her shame. Sadly, others have behaved more like the biblical teachers in John 8 who clearly relished the public condemnation of the woman caught in adultery. Like her, survivors may be forced to carry the shame that belongs to at least one other person.

It can be hard to understand it is not our own impurity, but the dirt of the abuser, which in the end is on the outside only, though it may feel as though it has penetrated deep into my soul. For Christians, the promise of salvation and new life in Christ offers a purification much sought and desired. It can be hard to accept, for in the cleansing there is also a scary revelation of the person hidden beneath the tarnish. It is harder still to understand that the abuser's impurity can never really defile me completely; as Jesus also said, what is unclean comes from the inside (the heart) not the outside and my heart is still uniquely my own (Matthew 15.1–20).

Lovelessness

Perhaps the most profound effect of all is the lack of love. It is the loss of an experience of good loving and therefore of a concept of what that is. It is the shutting down of the ability to love. It is more than recovering from the hurt or let-down – it is the complete collapse of even the basic certainties, the foundations that give most of us permission to leave the safety of our shell each day. It is like the shock of a trusted family dog of many years coming up to lick your face as usual and viciously biting it instead. You never trust the dog to be its usual self again. So how to trust a lover? Without trust love is hard to give or receive.

It can also be difficult to recognize and accept love that is offered without the conditions an abuser may have used. Being loved for whom I am, not how I perform, exposes me in all my vulnerability. If my self-image is distorted through the abuse and my self-esteem is at best fragile, at worst shattered, that vulnerable place is too terrifying to occupy. So the love most desired and most needed may be rejected because it is also too painful. Lovers need infinite stores of patience and wisdom to unfold the loveless child from the corner where she is hiding.

Learning to be loving to family, friends and to God presents a further challenge. Many survivors work very hard (and successfully) to create a loving home and set of relationships that contrast sharply with their own experience. Our desire and capacity to love have not been destroyed, but our aptitude may have been dented and we have not been taught or had full opportunity to practise the requisite skills. There is agreement within the range of disciplines working in the field of human development about the significance of attachment in building the capacity to love. A child's experience of forming a secure attachment to their primary care giver (normally their mother) is fundamental to their ability to form good relationships and to deal with life's traumatic events.

An abused child who has learnt not to trust that nourishment, touch, attention and care will come when needed and requested, eventually stops asking. This affects all aspects of healthy development and makes it exceptionally difficult to deal with any further trauma and abuse. In adulthood, someone abused as a child may struggle to connect emotionally and physically with other people, to form friendships, to reach and maintain the closeness of attachment that is fundamental to any loving relationship. In some survivors this difficulty is concealed behind a mask of mistrust that can appear cold or withdrawn, holding people at arm's length; in others it may be hidden by an apparent easy friendship that proves superficial or short-lived – if anyone starts to get too close we reject them or run away.

Boundary problems

Many survivors recognize that the experience of having boundaries violated, crossed or ignored leaves a legacy of boundary problems. In reaction it is common to swing to extremes rather than maintain a more balanced middle position: becoming a control freak or surrendering to others too early; saying yes to everything or no to everyone. Rejecting friendships or being too friendly too soon (then regretting and withdrawing suddenly). Boundaries have been violated and it takes time to re-learn to draw, hold and trust them again.

There are three key boundary areas I suggest are particularly important for survivors. The first is friendship; and I include family and partners as well as friends of either gender here. There are some qualities of friendship that can be distorted by abusive relationships, which need restoring to achieve healthy relationships, modelling the biblical agape of loving neighbour as oneself. The mystic Kahlil Gibran proposed 'Your friend is your needs answered' (Gibran, 1926, p. 69). An abuser has turned that round into a model of total self-sacrifice, and survivors may believe friendship has to be bought or earned, rather than freely offered. We frequently struggle to share the joys of friendship and to hold a balanced boundary between giving and receiving. The mutuality some believe is implicit in agape has not been our experience and it is hard to accept the good without the hesitation and suspicion that expects a friend will demand a payback. The survival instinct means we may be extremely self-sufficient, looking for little from other people (and therefore less hurt when expectations are disappointed); sadly this detachment, while an understandable protection at the time, also leads to isolation and others may experience us as withdrawn and unresponsive.

The second is the area of professional relationships. Many survivors function extremely effectively in their working context but overwork and stress are not uncommon. Work may be a safer place than home and here there is more control over role and function. A compassionate desire to serve others, prompted by the negative experiences of the abuse, may lead to overwork as we struggle to accept we cannot change all the evil ways of the world; or it may be a symptom of our inability to value and care for ourselves. This can lead to stress and associated mental health issues; or the temptation to look to our work and those we work with (both colleagues and 'clients') for all our needs. There is a danger here of repeating the unhealthy boundaries of the past and blurring the distinction between the personal and the professional: so I may not give due attention to my family and social life outside work; or I may develop an inappropriate dependency on my colleagues or clients for the approval, affirmation, status and affection we all seek. Some survivors may need good supervision to ensure boundaries are re-positioned appropriately. With clear self-awareness, others are excellent boundary-keepers, sharply focused on learning and applying the lessons from the abuser's own ambiguity in this respect.

Lastly there is the boundary of myself and my environment. Particularly for those abused as children, there are issues of identity arising from the insecure foundations on which I have formed my view of myself. I may need to re-draw the form that is the expression of my identity, so that the abuse is no longer at its core or foundation. During the abuse it was safest to be a chameleon, changing shape to fit the demands of the abuser. I may have split off different aspects of myself to create places of safety where they could be expressed; to the outside world these appear as different masks, in extreme cases they may be expressed as distinct personality states (see later section on 'dissociation'). A key task of healing becomes creating a unified boundary of self that retains integrity in all contexts.

Related to this is the capacity to control my environment. The lack of control during the abuse can create a control freak, who gives others a hard time in order to achieve the order and perfection that compensates for the powerlessness of the abuse. Others remain in helpless passivity, consumed by their environment and the whims of those around them. There is particular vulnerability here for further abuse, reinforced by the instinct to try to please those in authority that is the conditioned response of the victim. It will take time and much practice to locate a boundary that can deal with chaos and order, compliance and challenge, responsibility and delegation.

Sexual health

Relationship, love and trust issues can affect partnerships of any abuse survivors. Those who have experienced sexual abuse may have particular issues. Feelings of shame, being unclean, even revulsion make touch and intimacy difficult. Sex may be associated with pain, degradation, fear or forced obedience and may trigger flashbacks and nightmares. A body that experienced stimulation and even physical pleasure during the abuse, will be seen as a shameful betrayer. Sex may become an expected currency and normative pattern for relationships, leading to promiscuity; or may be seen as something obscene, to be avoided at all costs.

The utter vulnerability of a loving and committed sexual relationship is a gift we all deserve but also a threat to the self-protective instincts of most survivors. It needs that difficult offering of trust and opening of the hidden wounded self and it may take many years to find these possible. The patience of partners can be stretched meanwhile, and this demonstrates the importance of good support for them as well as for the survivor. Professional help may be needed to overcome the feeling of being unclean and the perception of sexual expression and touch as dirty and salacious; gentle understanding from partners and a very careful progression towards intimacy will be essential to restoring a healthy relationship.

Negative strategies

Increasingly the medical profession has recognized abuse as a major trauma, having effects on victims similar to those caused by other extreme events, including post-traumatic stress disorder (PTSD). There is a well-researched link between abuse and a significant number of people involved in mental health services and in prisons. The obvious conclusion is that for many survivors it is beyond our normal human resources to cope easily and well with what has happened to us and the wounds we have received. It is not surprising, then, that we adopt coping strategies which may also be negative in their effect, such as drug and alcohol misuse, eating disorders, self-injury and other types of self-harm. It is also not surprising that survivors suffer from depression, dissociation, obsessional and compulsive behaviour and other symptoms of mental unhealth.

It is beyond the scope of this book to deal with all of these areas in depth. Self-harm is considered further in Chapters 5 and 9, in both practical and theological frameworks. Here I just want to acknowledge that these are not in themselves the survivors' problems; they are emergent behaviours and issues from the underlying problem of the abuse and the damage it has caused. They can be seen as strategies adopted to deal with the unbearable; to restore health it is necessary to identify alternative positive coping strategies and work at transforming what can be changed of the underlying situation.

Mental distress

The organization MIND, which works in the interests of people with mental health issues, describes people with a mental illness as those 'experiencing problems with the way they think, feel or behave' (Stewart, 2000, p. 2). Many people suggest the term mental distress is perhaps a better way to describe the consequences of a wide range of influences on our mental well-being. Abuse is of course just one of these, but, as a traumatic experience, tends to have a most profound effect on the emotional health of victims and others closely affected. Many survivors and their supporters find that it is the mental or emotional effects that are the most enduring and hardest to deal with. It is unsurprising, therefore, to find that abuse victims form a high proportion of those accessing the various mental health services, and the majority of survivors report an experience of mental distress issues.

Dissociation

> Your sense of identity, reality and continuity depend on your feelings, thoughts, sensations, perceptions and memories. If these become 'disconnected' from each other, or don't register in your conscious mind, it changes your sense of who you are, your memories, and the way you see things around you. This is what happens during dissociation.
> (Livingston, 2002, p. 2)

All of us have some experience of dissociation or disconnection from our fully conscious selves – getting 'lost in thought' or those times when you drive home on automatic pilot and have no memory of the journey. In response to abuse or other extreme trauma, such as war or terrorism, this disconnection begins as a creative escape tactic but can become an obstacle to future well-being. Those working with people who have dissociative disorders now recognize that this is a survival strategy rather than an illness or personality disorder, and the previous term of 'multiple personality disorder' is no longer used. Of all mental health issues, dissociation perhaps responds best to treatment, particularly counselling and other talk-treatments.

There are different manifestations of dissociation and it is now generally recognized that there is a continuum of seriousness, from daydreaming to complex dissociative disorders. Symptoms may not be immediately obvious to either the person with the disorder or those around them, as dissociative people often put up a good front, and may also experience amnesia. They may share many of the symptoms common to PTSD, including flashbacks, out-of-body experiences, mood swings, derealization[2] and sleep disorders. Many will also use other negative coping strategies, such as drug or alcohol misuse.

Most research and those working in this field agree that dissociative disorders are directly linked to trauma or abuse; particularly 'repetitive, overwhelming, and often life-threatening trauma' in early childhood (Sidran, 2003, p. 3). Adult victims of major traumas including, for example, torture may use similar strategies; but children tend to be more expert in 'splitting off' so the defensive habit is more likely to be repeated in later daily life. Perhaps the biggest danger for any survivor is when the dissociative place remains more attractive and welcoming than the real world; obeying the inner imperative 'don't feel' excludes love, joy and excitement as well as fear and pain.

Of course it doesn't always have a negative effect. Meditative orders, from Christian mystics to Buddhist monks, strive to practise the same dissociation from daily reality in order to achieve a more developed spirituality. In a crisis, the ability to step out of the stress of the moment and maintain a calm focus and detached overview is a key skill for those called to deal with the situation. Christ the fugitive in Egypt, and the Jews who escaped from the same country so many generations earlier, surely understood the prudence of flight in extreme situations. (This theme is explored further in Chapter 9.)

Patterns of abuse

The previous chapter reported that there is no evidence that abuse victims grow into abusers. It is true that offenders report a higher than average history of abuse but no causal link has been proved. Indeed this is not surprising, given the possibilities for learnt and conditioned behaviour, the dynamics of post-traumatic stress disorder, the strain of the legacy of abuse and the lack of positive relationship models many victims face. There are some experiences that may be more likely to influence adult offending behaviour:

• People abused at a particularly young age are more likely to start abusing before adolescence and also to abuse younger children.

- Men who sexually abuse boys are more likely to report a history of child sexual abuse.
- High levels of violence and sexual deviancy within the family (whether witnessed or experienced) can contribute to developing abusive behaviour.
- Frequent changes in the main carer (e.g. because of maternal violence) can be a factor.

However, in the case of both sexual abuse and familial violence, the majority of victims do not go on to abuse; and the majority of offenders do not report a history of abuse. So there is no consistent causal link and there is a negligible risk that victims will become abusers in situations where they are in leadership. The practice in some churches, therefore, of banning adult survivors who disclose a history of abuse from working with children and vulnerable people, is discriminatory, unjust, unnecessary and itself abusive of a group of people with already fragile self-esteem and low confidence.

Struggles with faith

Because we strongly associate God with authority, love, parenting and care, all abuse has a potential impact on our relationship with God and the Church as the body of Christ. One of the victims of Chris Brain's abusive behaviour in the former Nine O'Clock Service is quoted (in Howard, 1996, p. 141) as saying: 'I still believe in a caring God, a creator, but I'm not interested in Jesus or church. Church turns God into something abusive.'

There are all the normal issues that anyone with a faith grapples with when something traumatic happens: Why me? Why so much suffering? Why didn't God rescue me? Was it my sin that caused the situation? Where was God when it happened? In addition there are issues heightened by the circumstances of the abuse, which will be particularly severe if the abuser is a minister or in another church leadership role. God as parent/creator/leader could betray our trust as our father/minister/partner did. Much as I long for God to be the good father I never had, I cannot easily relate to God as Father because of the bad conditioning of the past. Worse, there is some dubious or badly thought through simplistic theology that can make it sound like God wanted the abuse to happen: God demands sacrifices, God planned my life and made me as I am. (See Chapter 9 for more on abusive theology.)

Jeanette Gosney (2002) in talking about the experience of adult survivors of sexual abuse in the Church highlights the tensions many of our images of God create for survivors. God as (male) King may collide with our fear of the abuser; yet we also seek the 'good' Father of the Trinity. A holy immanent God is reassuringly trustworthy yet may be contaminated by our impurity. Jesus as Lover is scarily sexualized and intimate, yet also the tender relationship we yearn for.

Churches can be sacred places of healing and refuge for survivors, and some Christian communities are in the forefront of offering a healing space and advocacy on the justice issues. The average congregation, not yet so well informed, may unwittingly compound the damage the abuse has done through some of the rituals and doctrine that we take for granted. An emphasis on God as all-dominant, the hint of violence in some of the Christ-triumphant hymns, the explicit blood references in the communion service – all may trigger very nasty memories for many survivors. As with the awareness of the perspective of single-parent households, of people recently bereaved and of childless people on Mothering Sunday, it is not a question of changing the central message but of communicating inclusively and with sensitivity.

The area of theology that is most problematic is forgiveness. The imperative to forgive can become a burden to a survivor at any stage of the healing process; demanded too early and too easily, it will only have a negative effect as the permission to tell the story from the victim's perspective, express righteous anger and place responsibility firmly with the abuser is denied. Forgiveness is indeed a central theme in the arena of abuse but cannot be imposed or constructed. An alternative understanding of forgiveness is explored more fully in Chapter 5.

Effects of spiritual abuse

All survivors may struggle with some of the language and theology that appears to justify or minimize the abuse they have experienced, or suggests that God somehow condoned it. Those who have been abused spiritually or in any other way by those in ministry or church leadership have additional struggles to endure. Christians and churches that wish to deal responsibly with the victims of abuse within the church community need to take the time and effort to understand these particular issues and frame an informed and compassionate response.

I have already mentioned the core association with God as the ultimate figure of love and authority, now associated with abuse of trust. Where the abuser is a church minister or similar leadership figure, this is reinforced even more strongly. Only by listening to the particular experiences of survivors can we begin to gain an insight into the many variations of these associations. For example, someone sexually abused by a priest may find any form of touch, any reference to the body, or being a servant of the church, the 'handmaiden of the Lord', the sacrificial references in the Eucharist, all violently triggering and abhorrent.

Preparation for the [sexual] abuse often included lighting candles, ritual consumption of bread and wine and cutting the sign of the cross onto my lower stomach or pelvis as symbolic of the sacrifice I was about to make for God. I was reminded I was the handmaiden of the Lord and as such it was my calling and duty to serve the minister of the Lord in all his needs. Thus this coupling was both ordained and blessed by God. The wine and my blood mingled with Christ's sacrificial offering of himself, which I was about to echo. At the time I really believed this was ordained and, like medieval flagellation, the best way I could serve the Lord I loved. Once I began to understand the twisted reality of what had happened, church services and especially communion became places of torture for me. Here were blood-letting, pain, ritual sacrifices and servitude repeated and another man of the cloth that I was supposed to respect and, worse, receive bread and wine or touch from. I would freak out and cower at the back of the church or outside in the porch. People must have thought I was mad, but inside I was re-experiencing the physical pain of the cutting and the emotional struggle of trying to separate the good from the evil.[3]

Perhaps the biggest issue is the betrayal of trust and violation of boundaries by someone who represents not just their own but God's authority. There is a double whammy in this: as a victim, it's not just my belief in myself and in human nature that is affected, it is also my soul and my belief in God. The separation from self and from close relationships with others that many survivors experience is compounded by a separation from God.

Effects of ritual abuse

The elements of ritual as part of the abuse in the story quoted above bring a further dimension that link to a very complex and contentious area. The case above was abuse that involved ritual, but was within the context of one-to-one abuse; there is also the phenomenon of ritual abuse, involving regular abuses, with surrounding rituals, undertaken by a group of abusers and with multiple victims. There are professionals in all the key agencies – police, probation, health, social services, therapy – who accept the reality of ritual abuse and work to address the particular issues it raises. There are others who remain sceptical. I have been convinced through personal experience both of the reality of ritual abuse and of its variety of manifestations. For ritual abuse survivors, the language, codes and imagery of any religion, including Christianity, present huge obstacles. It needs a special community with good awareness and a developed sensitivity to enable ritual abuse survivors to feel safe enough to join. I think the biggest hurdle such survivors face is getting to tell their story. The tale is so unpleasant and shocking, it makes you feel ugly just to talk about it and you know that no one wants to listen; it's more comfortable for society to stay in denial. For the sake of justice, we need to be more prepared to hear the truth.

Effects on families

Abuse just refuses to be contained within the lives of the abuser and the victim. The effect ripples out as when a boulder (rather than a pebble) is thrown into a pond. Both during and after the abuse, the impact on other members of the family can raise many challenging issues. These will vary according to context, so the examples given represent just a freeze-frame of an ever-changing video.

In the context of sexual abuse, siblings may feel guilty because they are not also being abused; non-abusing parents may be avoiding facing suspicions due to an inability to deal with the implications. Afterwards siblings may discover that others were also being abused, and older children may feel guilty for not having protected younger siblings better. Sadly, parental denial can be a reaction to disclosure; it is not uncommon, for example, for a non-abusing mother to blame a victim daughter for the abuse by the step-father, and even kick her out of the house, in support for the partner-perpetrator. Or the abuse may have already spread within the family: an abusing mother may have been abused by her father, siblings may abuse each other, in a transference of power or because it is all they have known.

Even in the best of families any kind of abuse in any scenario is a devastating monster to deal with. The depth of raw emotions and the complicated web of damage take courage, patience, endurance and many years to disentangle and recover from. Initially, parents may find it hard to face the reality of what has happened and in an attempt to shield their children may fail to deal with vital issues, in effect silencing the victims once more. Attempting to cope with the harsh truth is an important step towards freedom.

Domestic violence isn't usually just towards wives; research demonstrates a high link (up to 66 per cent) with physical abuse of children, including further abuse during 76 per cent of contact visits (ordered by the court) after the parents have separated.[4] As part of the Economic and Social Research Council's (ESRC) Children 5–16 research programme, a rare study in April 2000 that focused on the children's *own* report of the effects on them discovered some significant themes. During the abuse, distress and fear are the most predominant responses; comfort may be found from siblings but many children remain alone with their feelings. Disruption to family life was a recurrent theme, from the immediate disruption of the abusive episodes to the geographical instability of frequent relocations. The main effects are of loss and displacement: of place, home, identity, treasured possessions, pets, friends, school and community. Coping strategies were many and varied and often displayed an advanced maturity. These ranged from hiding during the violence, to comforting mum after the abuse, to calling the police and direct intervention including protecting younger siblings. Remarkably, children 'understood that their mothers stayed with or returned to abusers due to concerns for their children's welfare' (ESRC, 2000). The children's plea was for people to be prepared to listen and believe them when they were trying to seek help, and for help and support during and after escape from an abusive situation.

Secondary victims

No family caught up in an episode of abuse escapes with just superficial damage. This is true whether the abuse takes place within the family or outside, whether relatives are understanding and supportive, or suspicious and scapegoat the victim. The same is also true for close friends and later partners of survivors. Families and friends will have their own concerns to deal with; each experience will be unique and will touch people in different ways, but some issues are common.

The first question asked is, What is the truth? Faced with such a horrifying situation, many may wonder whether it is real (because they wish it were not) and hesitate over exactly who to trust, with accusation and denial from different quarters. The further division, mistrust and hurt this causes compound the original abuse. It is worth reflecting that the abuser has everything to gain, and the victim all to lose, through weaving a fabric of lies. Then there is the problem of who to blame; even in the best of situations, where the victim's innocence is recognized, others may wrestle with the agony of whether there was more they could do to prevent the abuse occurring, or to intervene sooner. Oppressors create not just direct victims but guilty and impotent rescuers, among the many secondary victims.

The intense rollercoaster ride of emotions that abuse sets off is hard for everyone to deal with. The whole spectrum from shock, shame, guilt and anger through to grief may take hold in a rapid spiral or may continue at differing strengths for many years. Dealing with one another's feelings can be cathartic at times, at others an overwhelming burden. It is hard enough for the victim to find understanding and help in all this, especially if the family will not or cannot offer support. It is even harder for families and friends caught up in the fall-out, at the time or years later, to find resources to support them through the most testing times. Here is another area where churches could contribute to better practice (see Chapter 5).

The question of whether or not to report the abuse to the police or other appropriate authority may also cause division. Some Christian communities have been known to discourage such action, claiming it is the Christian way to forgive and move on, allowing the abuser to repent. The theological ideal may not be at fault, but its timing and application are disastrous. Those equipped and trained to do so are best able to investigate abuse just as any crime, such as theft or murder; and, I would suggest, are most likely to be those called by God to do so, just as we accept doctors are called to a healing vocation. (See Chapter 4 for guidance on reporting.)

If an official investigation is initiated, there are further issues to cope with. In my experience the key agencies today are generally well trained, sensitive and committed to good practice; which is not to say they get everything right all the time. But even in the best of scenarios, once the power of the agency takes over it can all feel very much out of control to the victim and everyone connected with the case. Where the investigation impacts on the wider community – for example, abuse within a church congregation or high-profile cases like the Soham murders – many other lives are touched and the ripples can stretch on for years. People will experience shock, fear, horror, anger and revulsion; they may retreat into denial and disbelief, take sides, have their own personal issues triggered, or try to remain outside and aloof from all that is happening. The victim and victim's family may feel overwhelmed, accused, judged, isolated, unsupported and burdened with responsibility. The legacy of distress and distrust may take generations to heal.

Historic abuse

It is not just at the time of the abuse that the consequences affect both survivors and their circle of relationships. It is not uncommon for someone to first disclose his or her experience of abuse many years after the event. The damage may have been well hidden and it comes as a violent shock; or the revelation may help to explain some behaviours and concerns. The timing seems to have little impact on the consequences: all the issues already discussed in this chapter can emerge days, months or years after the initial abusive act. For partners this represents a real challenge to steadfast love and commitment; there is a sense in which the agenda of the abuse can become dangerously dominant during the process of dealing with the effects. I am only too aware that my family and friends, over the years, have reaped some of the worst of the legacy and that my husband in particular has needed (and still needs) the patience of a saint to deal with my insecurity and fears, the compassion of a parent to tend my wounds, and the selflessness of an angel to accept the shared burden my experiences bring. As another husband of a survivor once commented, it can seem like the survivor's agenda drives the relationship, and while he understood the reasons behind that and in no way blamed his wife, he felt it would be nice sometimes to, say, do something on the spur of the moment without the abuse issues interfering (i.e. without constantly wondering if this was going to be triggering/dangerous/beyond what can be coped with that day, etc.). The hard truth in all this is that the ripples keep moving on, and no one – parents, children, friends, partners – is immune or protected from them.

It is hard coming out as a survivor. You might think we would get even more sympathy than a divorcee or someone made redundant. But often it is not a positive response; you are blanked or stonewalled, you can read the questions in the fear in people's eyes: are you going to turn into an abuser? Or a hysterical, clinging victim? Maybe you 'asked for it'? Isn't it time to put it all behind you? The disturbing, harrowing image of the cross that symbolizes a survivor's experience is not a comfortable place to pause; but there, where God is found in solidarity, is the place where our journey with survivors of abuse needs to start.

DISCUSSION QUESTIONS

To discuss
I have tried to communicate the reality of the experience of abuse from the survivor's perspective. What image stands out for you from the range of sensations and insights described? What have you learnt from this chapter? Will this change the way you respond to survivors in the future?

To reflect
I have suggested the crucifixion as the starting point of a journey of solidarity with survivors. Find a painting or artwork of the crucifixion and use it as the basis of a meditation. You might like to re-read the quote at the beginning of the chapter. How does Christ's experience of abuse speak to you? Where do you see God in the acts of abuse in our communities?

To do
Many survivors emphasize the power of being able to tell their story and know they have been heard. How can you create opportunities for survivors to share stories? What do you need to do to become a better listener?

Notes

1 Quote from a survivor, DR 2002, used with permission.
2 Derealization is a term used to describe a sense of the surrounding world seeming unreal and detached; it may also include items changing form in some way.
3 Quote from survivor, used with permission.
4 See <http://www.womensaid.org.uk/dv/childrensupdatedstats.html>.

References

Chevous, J., 'Breaking the Silence', *Third Way*, Vol. 26 No. 1, January/ February 2003.

Economic and Social Research Council (ESRC), Children 5–16 Research Programme Study, April 2000.

Gibran, K., *The Prophet*, William Heinemann Ltd., London, 1926 (1970 edn).

Gosney, J., *Surviving Child Sexual Abuse: Supporting Adults in the Church*, Grove Books, Cambridge, 2002.

Howard, R., *The Rise and Fall of the Nine O'Clock Service: A cult within the church?*, Mowbray, London, 1996. <http:www.womensaid.org.uk/ dv/childrensupdatedstats.htm>

Kershaw, C., Budd, T., Kinskott, G., Mattinson, J., Mayhew, P. and Myhill, A., *The British Crime Survey*, Home Office, London, 2000.

Livingston, K., *Understanding Dissociative Disorders*, Mind Publications, London, 2002.

Mitchell, Rebecca, 'Sexual Abuse – Helping to Heal', *Church of England Newspaper*, 23 October 2003.

Sidran Institute website, Dissociative Disorders, <http://www.sidran.org/ didbr.html> published Sidran 1995–2003, accessed January 2004.

Stewart, G., *Understanding Mental Illness*, Mind Publications, London, first published 1993, rev. edn 2000.

Wangerin, W., *The Book of God*, Lion Publishing, Oxford, 1996.

3

The Powerlessness Symphony: principles of a non-abusive culture

————◄○►————

In a recent work on supporting adult survivors of child sexual abuse, a framework of three movements is transcribed, creating a journey of healing (Gosney, 2002[1]). I used this symphonic framework in a previous article (Chevous, 2003) to compose a response to abuse that moves from the suffering of the cross to the hope of resurrection:

1 From diminution towards restoration
2 Isolation towards reconciliation
3 Domination towards liberation

A re-working of some movements of this symphony provides some core principles for creating a non-abusive culture, laying the foundations for the chapters that follow. Within this framework we can develop our response to abuse and practices aimed to prevent it, with the integrity of having attempted to deal with root causes.

1 Diminution towards restoration

Abusers have diminished both the victims and themselves – the profound reality of this is explored in Chapters 2 and 6. Our first movement is towards a restoration of original righteousness, the gift of God's grace to all that affirms our intrinsic worth. In musical terms, the refrain running through this movement is acknowledgement. We need to recognize and face up to the truth of abusive situations and ensure we hold abusers accountable for their actions. A common problem in handling disclosures of abuse is a perceived lack of honesty by the agency or church concerned. We may not want to hear what we are being told, so we tend to minimize the problem and its effects. We may find it hard to believe something so shocking, and be tempted to retreat into denial. We may be concerned about litigation and financial impli-cations, so are inclined to defend the institution rather than promote the common good. Such responses may be understandable; but in the context of abuse are collusive and lead to injustice.

It is not just the abuser and abused who are diminished. The other acknowledgement is of our own responsibility: for causing the abuse and for clearing up the mess. At one level this means examining the structures and relationships we have created to identify where they have supported, hidden and contributed to abuse and then taking steps to put things right. At the other it means living out the co-responsibility we have as one body, in our shared humanity and our shared participation in the Body of Christ: 'whatever you did for one of these brothers and sisters of mine, you did for me' (Matthew 25.40). In the context of examining original sin, McFadyen describes the interdependency of this for all of us: 'guilt is the responsibility for the joy of all before the lord of all'.[2] By acknowledging abuse as a structural sin that infiltrates all, contaminating the interdependent relationship of Creator and created, we bring an urgency and profound importance to our attempts to re-orientate ourselves towards God.

I suggest three principles that assist us to create a balance between mercy and justice – recognition, responsibility and restoration.

Recognition
We could heed Proverbs 26: 'smooth words may hide a wicked heart'. I believe that one of the reasons abuse continues is because we tend to minimize, excuse and therefore collude with abusers and their propensity to blame the victim or other people for their behaviour. When a charismatic leader abuses their power through subtle manipulation or destructive spiritual authority, we are too ready to accept what we see on the surface and ignore the devastation underneath. It is not surprising that it is much harder to accept the abuse on our doorstep than the distant cases we hear about through the media; but for the victim there are awful consequences. We cannot begin to deal with the problem until we are prepared to face uncomfortable reality with honesty. Abuse is always shocking, traumatic and, when it involves people that we know, tears apart our familiar picture of the world. It is easier to avoid or deny, holding on to the safety of the world as we thought we knew it. This helps none of us to find the truth. For victims in particular, acknowledgement of the reality of the abuse and the damage done is the first step towards dealing with the consequences.

Responsibility
Part of the distorted reality of abuse is the common transfer of responsibility from the perpetrator to the victim. This distortion needs to be corrected and the truth reinforced. Just as with any breakdown of positive human relationships, the community needs to take responsibility for dealing with the consequences, including, with historic abuse particularly, recognizing how previous silence, protection or disbelief may have contributed to the abuse. Since the Garden of Eden we have

understood that God expects us to face the consequences of our own actions. The woman accused of adultery was clearly directed to 'go and sin no more'. Where abuse is discovered, there must be a recognized procedure that deals with the perpetrators appropriately, including expecting them to acknowledge their responsibility. The Truth and Reconciliation Commission in South Africa was based on this model of granting an amnesty in return for full disclosure (Tutu, 1999).

Restoration

There is a model of restorative justice that moves from recognition and repentance through recompense to restitution. Chapters 5 and 6 consider further the difficult issues of forgiveness and working with offenders. Repentance in this context may be simply the opportunity for the wider family and community to demonstrate their solidarity with the victim and their sense of outrage and grief about what has taken place. Where our own leaders have been at fault, repentance should include a public as well as a private apology, a true acknowledgement of the wrong done. This provides the theme of the movement reciting the restoration of our community – shalom – that includes justice: 'There can be no peace without justice, and justice without love is brutality. Love without justice is weak sentimentality' (Otis Moss Jr, in Riley, 1995, p. 302). Recompense is not limited to money – Chapter 4 suggests many ways that people who have been abused can be supported. At best, it is identifying how to restore joy in damaged lives. Then 'restitution follows in seeking to repair the broken relationships and communities, accepting that there is no short cut or quick-fix process' (Chevous, 2003, p. 24).

2   Isolation towards reconciliation

The sustained bass line of the second movement emphasizes the danger of secrecy. Isolation is both a characteristic and a consequence of abuse. Open practice is a key note here, in a movement towards the unity of value and purpose that characterizes a reconciled community.

Community

Our most effective weapon against the dangers of secrecy and segregation is to create a community culture based on openness and honesty. If we separate ourselves too far from the rest of society, we ignore our interdependence with all our neighbours and create the perfect environment for incestuous practice to flourish. Chapters 6 and 7 will suggest some of the ways we can engage in good practice, networking effectively with our local community and thus holding ourselves accountable. This also brings new opportunities for Christian agencies to engage in mission and evangelism, and to support multi-agency and grass-roots initiatives to tackle the legacy and causes of abuse in our neighbour-hood. Inclusiveness is another refrain that we hear clearly in the model of radical community Jesus showed us. Sinners and the vulnerable were not just welcomed, but placed at the centre so that the quietest voices could be heard.

Transparency

Adopting working practices that are open and accessible for scrutiny also prevents the isolation of the individual. Guidelines for youth and children's workers that contribute to child protection, along with practices from professions facing similar issues, such as counsellors, teachers and doctors, can be adapted to the relevant areas of Christian organization (see Chapter 8). Transparency in the sense of self-awareness is also important and involves managing boundaries carefully. As Jesus instructed the Pharisees: 'first clean the inside of the cup and dish' (Matthew 23.26). Training for different ministries that expects a developed ability to reflect on one's own practice and recognize one's own agenda contributes to this 'cleaning', along with the accountability of regular supervision. Strategies for these areas are considered further in Chapters 7 and 8.

Reconciliation

A community that is in unity, rather than individualized, witnesses to reconciliation. It is the ultimate profound truth of the cross – we are reconciled to God through Christ, the broken relationship restored. Relationships that are lived out in equality, honesty and openness, witness to our great Christian truths of unity and harmony in creation. Archbishop Tutu describes the powerful witness of events in South Africa for other communities dealing with division and adversity: Northern Ireland, Rwanda, Israel. He emphasizes the vital place of forgiveness. It is a principle of Christianity and of social justice that is fundamental to achieving transformation, and the current tendency to demonize perpetrators of abuse is as destructive as the silencing of their victims. I will discuss the dangers of imposing forgiveness on an individual victim in Chapter 5; and develop an alternative theology of reconciliation in Chapter 9. The principle here is of community. We can share the burden and privilege of expressing forgiveness as a body, through due processes of investigation and holding to account. There is also the possibility of symbolic action, when the right time is reached to release the community from the legacy of abuse that has taken place and mark the next stage of the journey together. The experience of the Christian community in facilitating such gathered rituals, in public and perhaps for some families also in private, could be usefully applied here.

3   Domination towards liberation

Our third movement resonates again with the theme of restorative justice. 'Let justice be done to all mankind. If the strong oppress the weak, confusion and discontent will ever mark the path of man, but with love, faith, and charity towards all, the reign of peace and plenty will be heralded into the world – generations of men shall be called blessed' (Marcus Garvey, in Riley, 1995, p. 222). At the heart of our liberation melody are the notes of Henri Nouwen's 'wounded healer' – a model of vulnerable leadership. Love is also the fruit of our labours; restoring song to the silent and joy to the mourners.

Powerlessness

In Chapter 7 I will suggest that it is Jesus' model of exposed, servant leadership, the way of stable and cross, that best protects us from abuse and nurtures the skills and practices that overcome oppression. This is not to overlook the power of powerlessness, or to suggest that power in itself is corrupt. As Penny Jamieson concludes from her reflections on life as the first female Bishop in New Zealand, 'power with consent has the potential to foster identity and community and to be both productive and creative with positive results, as opposed to the inertia of negativity' (Jamieson, 1997, p. 11). She suggests it is not the location of power that is critical, but the exercise of it. An incarnational model that acknowledges the local and particular reflects the mutuality of the Trinity. This means that an individual 'holding power on behalf of the community . . . [can] work in a way that enables the members of the community to acknowledge their own power and their stake in the powerholder' (ibid., p. 12). In our response to abuse, this might best be lived out in the models of accompanying and advocacy described in the next two chapters. Perhaps the powerholder's most fundamental role is that of listener; this is especially key in ensuring that the voices of the powerless – survivors – are heard in all areas of the process. Their experience and its cost should be honoured in the formation of policy and the implementation of practice at all levels. What better experts do we have?

Joyfulness

How do we answer the culture of domination that gives its subtle permission to abusive leaders and individuals? Once more the image of joy resonates here, the fundamental activity of worship that McFadyen (2000) refers to. Chapter 9 explores how a theology of oppression could be transformed into a theology of joy. While there is beauty in truth, the joylessness that comes in the fall-out of abuse needs a proactive antidote. In Chapter 5, which focuses on the healing journey, there are suggestions for restoring joy into the lives of survivors. It is easy to get caught up in the agony and the angst of abuse, to remain dragged down in the slime at the bottom of the pit and forget to look up to the light. Yet there are so many simple ways to rekindle the smouldering wick of hope; the childish pleasures of play and delight in creation, the companionship of hospitality and solicitous care. Our responses should be measured not just by their truthfulness and justness but also by their capacity to bring love.

Liberation

'The God we know in the Bible, is a liberating God . . . a God who intervenes in history in order to break down structures of injustice and who raises up prophets in order to point out the way of justice.'[3] The liberation of our communities from the oppression of abuse is the *shalom* that Jesus restored for us. Perry Yoda[4] talks about 3 dimensions of shalom:

1 *Well-being: health and material prosperity.* The aim of the suggestions in this book is to restore good health for the abused, the abusers and their surrounding community. This encompasses mental, physical, emotional and spiritual well-being. Addressing the diseases of social exclusion – poverty, oppression, homelessness – is an inextricable part of creating prosperity. Finally there is the principle of bounteousness – ensuring the resources needed to support good practice are freely and generously available, without resort to litigation or political protest.

2 *Right relationships: peace, justice and the removal of oppression.* Abuse of power at any level of relationship is clearly a strong strand in the fabric of oppression that cloaks our world. I understand the Christian calling to prioritize the liberation of restored relationship in God's here and now Kingdom, an echo of our eschatological hope of God's perfect Kingdom beyond this world.

3 *Straightforwardness: honesty and moral integrity.* Seekers of truth (with its promised liberation: 'the truth shall set you free') follow the way of truth. Jesus' anger and condemnation were most often aimed at hypocrisy, itself an abuse of power and characterized by moral dishonesty. We cannot, of course, know all truth, and at best attempt to draw together a patchwork of pieces, hoping to recognize the pattern. Perhaps the integrity is in the journeying not the arriving: 'in order to know truly we need to want to exercise power rightly' (Volf, 1996, p. 299). In the dialogue of truth-seeking, this might mean relinquishing my own truth in order to give space for yours. For survivors, it is often their truth that has been silenced; but redressing the balance must also enable all perspectives on the truth to surface.

Each of these qualities of shalom echoes the themes we have played in our symphony for prevention, re-orientating us towards joyful relationship with each other, God and the whole of creation. It is a movement beyond justice to embrace 'love *shaping* the very content of justice' (Volf, 1996, p. 220). It is this hopeful music that sustains and energizes survivors like myself to continue to break the silence.

DISCUSSION QUESTIONS

To discuss
I have suggested a number of qualities that should feature in a non-abusive culture. Which of those recommended do you think is most important? What other qualities would you look for?

To reflect
A theology of oppression is contrasted with a theology of joy. When do you play with God? How do you experience the joy that God offers? What brings you joy?

To do
I suggest that reconciliation can transform communities that have experienced abuse. Where do you see division and adversity in your community? Where are there attempts to effect reconciliation? How can you be a peacemaker?

Notes

1 Total credit to Jeanette Gosney for the inspired framework headings; I bear full responsibility for the rest!
2 McFadyen, 2000, p. 248, with apologies for my simplistic interpretation of his rich theological engagement.
3 Emilio Castro, *Amidst Revolution*, quoted in Roger Sainsbury, *Justice on the Agenda* (1985).
4 Quoted by Howard Zehr in his book on restorative justice, *Changing Lenses* (1990).

References

Chevous, Jane, 'Breaking the Silence', *Third Way*, Vol. 26 No. 1, January/February 2003.
Gosney, Jeanette, *Surviving Child Sexual Abuse: Supporting Adults in the Church*, Grove Books, Cambridge, 2002.
Jamieson, P., *Living at the Edge: Sacrament and solidarity in leadership*, Mowbray, London, 1997.
McFadyen, A., *Bound to Sin: Abuse, Holocaust and the Christian Doctrine of Sin*, Cambridge University Press, Cambridge, 2000.
Riley, D. W. (ed.), *My Soul Looks Back, 'Less I Forget: A collection of quotations by people of color*, Harper Perennial, New York, 1995.
Sainsbury, Roger, *Justice on the Agenda*, Basingstoke, Marshalls, 1985.
Tutu, Desmond, *No Future Without Forgiveness*, Rider, London, 1999.
Volf, M., *Exclusion and Embrace: A theological exploration of identity, otherness and reconciliation*, Abingdon Press, Nashville, 1996.
Zehr, H., *Changing Lenses: A New Focus for Crime and Justice*, Herald Press, Scottdale, PA, 1990.

4

Embracing the Truth: how to handle incidents of abuse

————◄○►————

> Woe to you, teachers of the law and Pharisees, you hypocrites! You are
> like whitewashed tombs, which look beautiful on the outside but on the
> inside are full of the bones of the dead and everything unclean. In the
> same way, on the outside you appear to people as righteous but on the
> inside you are full of hypocrisy and wickedness.
>
> Matthew 23.27–28

This chapter aims to provide resources for improving our practice in
responding to abuse where we recognize it. The starting point is the
recognition of our shared responsibility to deal with the consequences
of abuse, not just out of neighbourliness, but because we do all share a
responsibility for allowing abuse to continue: through our inaction or
inappropriate action, our avoidance or tendency to scapegoat, and
through our theology of domination. The implications of the principles
explored in Chapter 3 are applied in processes to deal with abuse; while
there are some specific procedures relating to abuse of children, the
underlying principles apply to all contexts, including reports of historic
abuse and abuse of adults who are vulnerable due to the power
dynamics of a relationship (e.g. pastoral and spiritual abuse) or due to
age, learning disability, mental distress, etc.

We are all aware of the growing tide of disclosures within major
caring institutions, of unrecognized or silenced abuse of some of the
most vulnerable groups in our community – children, the elderly,
disabled people – only now revealed by adults, often many years after
the event.[1] The Church has not been immune to this; in fact it has been
on the tail end of both recognizing the extent of the problem, acknowledging the reality, and finding appropriate ways to deal with it. The
Protestant churches in England may be breathing a slightly guilty sigh
of relief that the Catholic Church in the USA seems to have suffered
from this 'phenomenon' far more than us. My own experience and the

little research available suggests we are beginning to see the floodgates open here as well.

An active campaigner in Australia recently summarized a typical poor organizational response (Henderson, 2002):

- victim seeks acknowledgement, apology, counselling
- Church authorities initially sympathetic but no action (long timescale)
- Church concludes 'investigation' but claims allegations not substantiated
- victim initiates civil action
- Church agrees out-of-court money settlement with gagging order

The impression that the Church then gives – sadly correct – is that the institution is more important than the victim. We know that something went wrong, but because in such cases it is hard to establish proof, we are afraid of litigation and financial costs, so we protect our interests above all others. We are not acting with love towards either the victim (who needs compassion) or the perpetrator (who needs discipline). We are not dispensing care or justice.

In the Church of England, my own experience of trying to report the sexual abuse I had suffered at the hands of an ordained priest over many years, as a young adult, is reflected in the experience of other survivors:

> The Church has not responded. A year ago, I took the terrifying step of reporting Mike to his current bishop. I told my story, and it was suggested that I meet with Mike, either alone or with the Bishop or another present. The idea appeared to be to effect reconciliation, or to test the credibility of my allegations. I declined, as Mike had written to me denying the abuse and threatening legal action – it seemed pointless and felt very unsafe. The only option offered continued to be a meeting, with someone who was not even acknowledging what he had done. I told the Bishop that I just wanted the appropriate steps to be taken to address his professional misconduct and ensure Mike was not abusing anyone else. I just wanted to be heard, I wasn't strong enough to be part of the solution. I was aggressively told off for being 'judge, jury and executioner'. It was suggested I could report him for rape. But I had no desire to drag all of us through a messy court case. So a year on, and a few curt letters later, nothing has happened. No healing, no justice, not even pastoral concern. No breaking of the silence.[2]

The way of truth explored in this chapter may seem a higher-risk option, but in fact is the only way that can lead towards the best consequence for everyone involved. Good practice should follow the principles already described, of honest recognition, facing responsibility and seeking restoration. The recent report on dealing with sexual abuse commissioned by the Churches Together in Britain and Ireland provides a thorough examination of good practice and has supported current initiatives by the major denominations to establish their own procedures. Any initiative is to be welcomed, although some areas prompt a lukewarm rather than enthusiastic response.

Every church and agency should adopt a policy and appropriate procedures for dealing with disclosures or suspicions of abuse. In many situations, the denominational headquarters or national body will have issued guidelines for these. Alternatively, you can seek advice from national bodies such as (in the case of child abuse) the Churches' Child Protection Advisory Service or from local agencies such as the Area Child Protection Committee of the Local Authority. Such agencies are also able to approve individual policies, give advice on good practice in particular situations, provide training for staff and offer support during and after a disclosure. Most major denominations and national agencies have recently made good progress in this area, and this chapter underlines their good practice and calls for the voice of the survivor to be sustained more clearly in the process. As the Climbié Inquiry highlighted, and recent examples of spiritual abuse confirm, it is the smaller and independent church movements and organizations that are least prepared and therefore most vulnerable. What follows aims to provide essential tools for establishing the basics of a good response.

Tuning up: good preparation

There are three ways that you can become aware of a situation of abuse:

- Experience – you realize you are being abused. I will deal with reporting your own experience later in the chapter.
- Disclosure – the victim(s) or someone else tells you about it.
- Observation – your suspicions are aroused by behaviour, incidents, injuries or conversations that you have seen or heard.

The information may include suspicions and allegations from both children and adults about abuse of both children and adults, either historic incidents or abuse that is still taking place. In all cases there is a need both to respond to those affected and take appropriate action to ensure that there is not a continuing risk to known victims or others in contact with the abuser. It is important that however the abuse comes to your attention, you take it seriously and respond according to appropriate good practice.

There are specialist organizations dealing with most contexts of abuse (see Chapter 10 for some suggested contacts). When it comes to abuse of adults by those in leadership or with pastoral responsibility, sources of support are less clear. In most situations, good grievance and disciplinary policies, supported by ethical policies or codes of conduct, will provide an adequate procedural framework. This can be supplemented by giving consideration to the particular issues raised by the abuse scenarios most likely to be faced within each environment. For example, a counselling team will need a different ethical code to a youth or children's organization, while the latter will need to pay greater attention to creating a child-orientated complaints procedure and to developing advocacy skills. Some key specific examples are given towards the end of this chapter.

Any church or agency should consider taking the following steps to ensure it is adequately prepared for dealing with abuse disclosures:

1 Establish comprehensive local and national networks with the key agencies working with abuse issues.
2 Adopt appropriate polices and procedures and ensure staff, volunteers, members and users are aware of these and equipped to implement them.
3 Consider the core principles underpinning any policy response and check that these are upheld in the spirit rather than the letter.
4 Plan to provide access to appropriate support for everyone affected by a disclosure both during and after any investigation.

Good preparation will create a more beneficial response and prevent mistakes that only compound the abuse and its effects. In this area there is some good practice emerging from a number of Christian institutions, and this can be more widely adopted. It is important to check with any federation head, denominational headquarters or umbrella body you belong to whether there is already some procedure in place and how it is being implemented. Only in delivery does a policy become effective. It is equally important to resource and monitor implementation in order to maintain good standards and identify any necessary review.

Initial disclosure

The following sections deal in general terms with the process of dealing with disclosures and discoveries of abuse, highlighting tricky issues and suggesting best practice. Particular issues pertinent to specific situations, such as child abuse, are highlighted separately towards the end.

Believe in the story
If this is a disclosure, do not be sidetracked by the fear of false allegations. I am puzzled as to why this myth has been perpetuated by

apparently fair-minded and intelligent people. In what other context do we promote the assumption that people are more likely to be deliberately lying? Chapter 2 explored how daunting and arduous it is for a victim to even *begin* to tell. Evidence and experience demonstrate that there is seldom anything to gain from false allegations and normally some foundation to the report; even if the story has been changed to make it easier to tell.[3] Anyone disclosing abuse is a person seeking to be heard and needing assistance. In my experience, telling is so traumatic you have to be desperate to go through with it – only a masochist would do it for fun and only strong evidence enables a case to proceed. The re-abuse of disbelief is too high a price to pay for protecting professional reputations.

Identify the process
Different contexts of abuse will need to be dealt with through different procedures. A disclosure of child abuse that might indicate a child is still at risk of significant harm must be followed through with the proper child protection procedures. Abuse of trust within a professional relationship, such as by a minister, will be the subject of a complaints or grievance procedure. Domestic violence and rape are criminal matters and our role becomes one of advocacy and support.

Careful investigation

Often this means bringing in the agency with the appropriate training and experience to undertake the investigation.

Qualifications
We are not always equipped to undertake an investigation and can cause significant damage if we try to do so. Particularly if there is the potential of future litigation, a badly handled investigation can destroy crucial evidence. A thorough investigation, undertaken with a transparent process that people can trust, makes it easier also to trust the truth of the outcomes (and therefore reduce the fear of miscarriages of justice). Good practice should include the careful recording of observations and conversations regarding the abuse, signed, dated and kept in appropriate secure and confidential storage.

Internal investigations
When it comes to abuse committed within our organization, we will normally have a key responsibility for investigation. This may not be able to proceed until any criminal investigation has been completed; the agencies concerned will give advice about this. Of course not all abuse sustains criminal or civil complaints. There may not have been a crime committed within the current legislative framework, or there may not be

sufficient evidence to proceed to prosecution. Neither necessarily means there is no case to answer, only that either there is no police investigation or the results are inconclusive and don't come to court. Often there will be some guidance or helpful information from the statutory bodies about how we should proceed. The challenge comes when we have to take responsibility for investigating on our own. Not many leaders or managers are well trained in this area and none of us likes making significant judgements that carry such a weight of responsibility. It is tempting to try to rush a process through as quickly as possible with the risk that our judgements may be hasty, ill considered and not owned by all concerned. Another temptation is to avoid the issue altogether or to attempt to move straight to a debate about reconciliation. The trouble with this is that, by default, the victim is denied the opportunity to be heard and to see justice being done; and the perpetrator does not have the opportunity to have their perspective understood, and to take responsibility for what they have done. It is not only unjust but also does not present the best possibility for grace and redemption.

Considering evidence

One of the normal requirements of English civil and criminal law, and most disciplinary procedures, is for sufficient evidence to corroborate a complaint. In cases of abuse it is not always easy for the victim to gather such evidence, as the abuse normally happens in secret and the abuser frequently takes steps to ensure there is no clear evidence to expose what is happening. This presents us with a significant dilemma in seeking the truth; Solomon's wisdom is needed when there is just one word against another's. To make an assumption of either guilt or innocence is clearly unjust to either side. For a victim to have the responsibility of proving the other's guilt is no better than the accused having to prove their innocence. I am struck by the thought that in that very situation, Jesus remained silent.

Education and training

It is much easier to interpret information accurately when we have a greater understanding of what we are hearing. The enlightened witness model is based on the experience that abuse is difficult to recognize from outside as well as from inside a situation. However, there are recognizable patterns of behaviour and effect and if we undertake a programme of education that raises our knowledge of abusive practice, we are more likely to recognize the evidence that is there and interpret it correctly.

Transparency in decision-making

A process that is undertaken in the open and with clear routes of accountability and accessibility is a process that all parties can trust and have confidence in. It may be that initial investigation needs to protect anonymity and to protect innocence wherever it sits. That does not prevent the actual process from being transparent if the work is done to ensure that there is consultation in its conception and delivery, that all parties are clear how they can access and influence the proceedings and that all the appropriate information will be made public once a decision has been reached.

Impartiality

Although at one level I would accept the argument that none of us is impartial – due to our cultural, genetic and environmental heritage – there are different degrees of subjectivity that it is important to recognize. We observed in 'Mike's' case above how it was understandably easy for the Church, carrying out its own investigation, to be pulled into defending its employee over a 'service user' and its own position and integrity as an institution. Most procedures at least ensure that the person (or group) who undertakes the investigation, the one who makes the decision and the one who hears any appeal are three separate bodies. It is possible to take this a step further by involving a consultant or impartial observer who is not part of the institutional authority. As Benyei (1998) suggests, the role of this person is not to impose solutions from outside, but to gather as thorough and truthful a picture of the situation as possible; then accompany the organization towards a place of shalom.

Probability

The general trend in professional disciplinary hearings is to move towards a standard of proof that reflects the level sought in civil rather than criminal proceedings. That is, rather than on the higher standard that it has been proved 'beyond reasonable doubt', decision-makers believe on a balance of probability that the abuse has taken place. The two standard tests of probability are: first, that the evidence is more likely to be true (51 per cent) than untrue, and second, that the victim's evidence is more probably true than any evidence supplied by any other party (which may contradict it).[4] Adopting this standard in cases of abuse means it is more possible for a victim to demonstrate a probability that the abuse took place. For example, counselling records, diary entries, medical records, logged previous concerns about the alleged perpetrator, character witness testimony and expert testimony may demonstrate the likelihood that a victim's testimony is indicative of abuse, even when the abuse has not been observed directly by any third party. This is where it becomes particularly important that the people making the decision have sufficient training to interpret correctly the information they are given.

Advocacy and empowerment

It is easy for systems and agencies to take over and for the person who has been abused to experience a strong echo of the lack of control and the overwhelming of the original abuse.

Whether child or adult, they need a good advocate to walk alongside them during the whole process, helping them to work out what they want to do, to ensure their voice is heard and sometimes, when they are not at a place to do so, to represent their viewpoint. We can be too quick to rescue or to offer our solutions; we risk disempowering victims further when we assume that we know what is best for them. Even with child protection issues, it is normally possible, for example, to support victims in reporting for themselves rather than rushing in to involve the statutory agencies before the victim is ready.

One area where current practice could be improved is in ensuring that the voices of those most concerned are heard in the procedures being set up. The good practice learnt from the self-advocacy movements, for example those working with young people and children in local authority care, and with people with learning disabilities, highlights the importance of not losing the voice of the victim within the professionalization of procedures. Youth-work practice, with successful models of empowering young people to participate fully in decision-making and community governance, is also a good resource. The committees we set up to create and implement policy and procedures should include survivors' voices, people with personal experience of the issues, not just professionals who have to act in the 'best interest' which may not fully appreciate the perspective of those most deeply affected by their decisions. This is particularly important within any complaints procedure, ensuring that survivors can trust the process and truly believe that their voices will be heard and understood.

Support

My own experience of reporting abuse through official Church channels highlighted the 'support lottery' in such situations. In that particular case, there appeared to be reasonable support for the perpetrator but none for the victim. In another (fostering), the opposite scenario took place, of good support for the victim and none for the alleged perpetrator. Clearly it is important that both are considered and appropriate independent support offered to both parties. A pool of trained and supervised supporters would be an essential resource for any organization. For some smaller groups and congregations, this might be difficult to achieve without help; this is where larger groups can provide vital practical assistance. It is particularly important that different people are responsible for supporting victim and alleged perpetrator, as there is a potential conflict of interest, whether or not the disclosure of abuse is accepted or denied. It is an example of the way a community process of justice can hold together different issues in a way an individual focus cannot. This can be helpful in lifting us beyond an adversarial model (based on accusation and denial) to an inquisitorial approach (seeking the truth from a 360 degree perspective).

Mediation

The experience with reporting 'Mike' appeared to rush into a suggestion of mediation leading to reconciliation before the processes of telling, investigation and decision-making about the truth of the situation had occurred. The victim needed to be heard first and he was still in denial. This was not a good place to start a reconciliation attempt. I suggest that mediation is not an alternative to the process of seeking justice, but may be an appropriate way to deal with the consequences. Many of the issues concerned with this are discussed in detail in Chapter 6. The essence of mediation follows my key principles, of sharing the stories in order to discover a shared truth. But this is only one step towards justice. Fundamentally, mediation is a process designed to enable conflicting parties to communicate before moving forward together (such as in family welfare proceedings or conflict resolution). In the context of abuse, bringing together the victim and abuser removes responsibility from the community for their part in resolving the situation. It also takes no account of the power dynamics and the potential for the abuser to re-abuse within the mediation attempt. The National Family Mediation (NFM) network defines mediation as 'directly negotiating your own decisions with the help of a third party. It is an alternative to solicitors negotiating for you or having decisions made for you by the courts. Entering mediation is always voluntary' (NFM, 2004). This suggests to me two equal parties sorting out their own lives without unnecessary intervention. In the case of abuse, this is rarely a possibility.

Pastoral care

The strong tendrils of abuse are far-reaching and hook into deep and raw emotions. It is important to establish an effective net of pastoral care for everyone affected. Support for survivors is considered in the next chapter. It is also important to consider what care is needed by the other groups involved.

Alleged perpetrators
It should be easier for Christian organizations to understand and follow the dual principles of justice and mercy. Both during and after investigation, perpetrators of abuse still need counsel and support. To avoid

duplicity and complicity, it is important that a suitably trained person offers this. Equally essentially, it should not be the same person who is supporting the victim.

The families involved

Parents, partners, siblings, children and the extended family of both the victim and perpetrator will have their lives turned upside down by the disclosure. They may react in a host of different ways, including anger, denial, blame, guilt, shame, grief and bewilderment. Even families with strong relationships and good internal resources will struggle to deal with all the issues on their own. A family already weakened by dysfunctional relationships or other 'baggage' can be torn apart. In a church or caring agency, consider preparing a team of trained 'listeners' who can support people through the investigation and beyond. This is where the preparation of a good referral network demonstrates its value.

The staff team concerned

Whether the abuse has taken place within the agency or not, and whether it is a current situation or happened many years ago, the staff will find this a challenging situation to work through, whatever their role. Normal staff support systems may need to be enhanced, in order to offer a safety valve, a listening ear and appropriate guidance to all staff. It is important to recognize that people with personal experience of abuse may find that the emotions and issues surrounding their own experience will be triggered by dealing with this new event and they may need to access professional support themselves. Equally, it can be traumatizing and stressful dealing with others' painful stories and strong emotions; at the very least, staff will need a safe-space to off-load.

The wider community

Once the story is first told, abuse cannot stay secret for very long. How widely the story becomes known will depend very much on the nature and context of the abuse in each case. It may be only the families and professionals involved who know. It may be that a large group need to be interviewed as part of a complex investigation. However good the confidentiality process, word will spread. This is good, in that openness promotes truth and the possibility of justice. It is problematic in that the dynamics of those immediately concerned will be replicated within the wider body. Friends and acquaintances will be shocked, upset and fearful. Some will get drawn into the investigation and its consequences. People will take sides. If the perpetrator is in leadership, there is a sense in which everyone will feel violated and abused. Coming to terms with issues of abuse is similar to a shared experience of grief, for example when a school pupil dies. The whole community need support to deal with the issues and emotions they encounter which are not part of the world they normally expect to inhabit.

Reporting child abuse

I need to emphasize again, that each church or agency should have its own procedures, which may be informed by local or national policy relating to the denomination or agency affiliation. Because these agreed protocols can be specific to the organization and need to be informed by the latest statutory guidance, it is inappropriate to provide a detailed model here. (See Appendix 1 for a summary of the standard procedure currently operating.) Below I give an overview of the core process that currently features in any procedure based on best practice. The results of the inquiry into the death of Victoria Climbié and the lessons from the Ian Huntley case are leading to significant changes in child protection practice; information given here should be verified with the appropriate agencies to ensure that the most up-to-date procedures are followed.

Duty to report

If you have concerns about a child or young person, you should report it by informing one of the bodies with a statutory duty to investigate child abuse. This should be done wherever possible *with* the young person rather than for them or behind their back; but the duty to act if a child is at risk of significant harm is overriding. The proposed new Local Safeguarding Children Boards will undoubtedly bring changes; in the meantime there are three routes you can take:

1 Call your local Social Services Department (ring the local council and ask to be put through to the Social Services Child Protection Team – an 'on-call' service normally operates outside of office hours).
2 Call the NSPCC on 0808 800 500 (24-hour line).
3 Call your local Police and ask to speak to the Child Protection Team.
4 In addition local procedures may require you to contact your organization or denomination's child protection specialist.

Investigation

What happens next is determined by the law and procedures set out in the Children Act 1989 and subsequent guidance such as *Working Together to Safeguard Children* (1999) and *Framework for the Assessment of Children in Need and their Families* (2000). The green paper *Every Child Matters* (2003) and the new Children's Bill (2004) signal some new practice to come when the Bill is implemented. These establish core principles for child protection including:

- The welfare of the child (or young person) is paramount.
- The wishes and feelings of the child, when possible, should be ascertained and taken into account. The child should be involved in the process.
- Social Services must work in partnership with families (unless it is contrary to the child's welfare).
- There should be a multi-disciplinary approach to what happens (i.e. involving schools, health professionals, youth workers, churches).
- Information-sharing is key to protecting children from harm but needs to respect the individual's rights to privacy and self-determination.
- The assessment of the child's situation should be holistic, taking into account the child's needs, the family's capacity to care for the child, and environmental factors (community resources, housing, income, family history and functioning).

Follow-up

You should ask to be kept informed of how your referral will be progressed so that you can support the child or young person concerned. Appendix 2 provides an outline of what happens after you refer a case of potential child abuse; this is the procedure set out by the government as *good practice*. Sadly, good practice does not always happen. In recognition of this, the government now expects Social Services to advise children and their families of their right to independent support and advocacy when going through the Child Protection/Social Services system. Organizations such as Voice for the Child in Care have developed a free independent advocacy service (see Resources section in Chapter 10).[5]

Key lessons

A key lesson for the Church from the Climbié Inquiry is to recognize how we can give permission to abuse through our ignorant good intentions and lack of accountability to others.[6] The immediately obvious conclusions from the Ian Huntley case are that it is crucial to share information that identifies a significant risk of harm and to make sure that the systems set up on paper are realistic, effective and implemented on the ground. Important principles for the future emerge from evaluating these past mistakes:

1 Educate staff, volunteers and members of churches and organizations thoroughly in understanding the complex and invasive nature of abuse, the implications of inappropriate action and the correct procedures to follow.

2 Inter-agency co-operation *that works on the ground* is vital to successful child protection. The Church cannot handle these issues

alone and has an important role to play with other agencies. We should develop local networks that establish effective information-sharing and referral routes.

3 Too strong a pair of theological sunglasses can distort our perception of what should be an obvious reality. Our concept of evil and sin should not blind us to the extent that clear indications of child abuse are misinterpreted as disturbed behaviour or possession. Spiritual warfare does not *replace* the need for counteracting human sin with human justice and care.

The child's voice

The final and perhaps most vital lesson in all child protection is the need for the child or young person to have their voice heard and protected. Too often every agenda is driven by the needs and perceptions of the adults: considering the needs of the whole community, or our spiritual agenda or professional reputation, aiming to reduce pressure from the media and 'the mob'. In all this, where is the voice of the victim? Her deepest needs and desires don't often match our adult theological, professional or litigation-aware framework. We are concerned to do the right thing by everybody; she longs for reassurance that she isn't worthless and responsible. We are anxious to be seen to be acting correctly; he needs the sanctuary of a safe hiding and healing space. Our justice demands a complex investigation that puts her on trial with the abuser; she just wants it all to stop.

The role of advocate – explored further in the next chapter – is one that churches and independent caring agencies could provide throughout a child protection investigation and beyond. It is perhaps the most important role and one that non-statutory bodies are best equipped to provide. However caring and committed a social worker or police officer may be, their very role in the system ensures they are not just able to be concerned with the child's agenda. The 'best interest' of the child – to be kept safe, away from the abuser – may conflict with the child's desire for the family to stay together. It is of course right that there is a justice system that considers the wider picture, but within it all if we can support the victim to break out of his or her silence, we will be paying attention to the most important and vulnerable person, who has, like Christ, paid the highest price.

Abuse of power against adults

Abuse of power by people in leadership or authority positions, or roles of trust such as counsellor or priest, is always an abuse of trust but may not lead to a criminal or civil legal action. It is a disappointment to campaigners that the Sexual Offences Act 2003 legislated for abuse of trust (in relation to sexual abuse) for people under the age of 18, or adults with specific mental illnesses or learning disabilities, within strictly defined relationships such as carers in residential homes. The wider range of cases of known abuses of all kinds in situations as diverse as counselling to hospital care, pastoral visiting to holiday missions, are not covered by legislation, only by professional guidelines. So it is even more important for the victim of the abuse that there is an effective professional and organizational process (such as an accessible and transparent complaints procedure) to deal with his or her disclosure. There remains the danger of unstructured and unregistered bodies, such as independent counselling centres, which do not come under any national regulatory process. Concerns have recently been raised about such a centre in another European country, but there is no agency willing to take responsibility for investigation. The final recourse remains unofficial grass-roots action: media campaigns, boycotts and local protest – a path previously trodden by whistle-blowers, but not an easy one.

Dealing with historic abuse

There are some particular issues to consider facing historic abuse cases. The first principle of belief in the evidence is especially sensitive here. On the one hand the events took place a long time ago and it may be hard to gain an immediately clear picture of what took place. On the other hand, it is entirely possible that the first victim to come forward may lead to the discovery of other victims; and the person implicated may still be in leadership. This is not something that can be undertaken lightly or easily.

Age factor
If the disclosed abuse took place when the victim was a child under 18, it becomes a child protection issue, however long ago it happened, and the police should be contacted to undertake the investigation. As with all occasions when the statutory agencies are to be involved, it is more empowering for the survivor if you support them to make the initial contact themselves, when they are ready. However, if they are reluctant to do so but the information you have suggests children and young people may still be at risk – for example the person is still employed as a youth leader or minister – then you have a responsibility to report anyway. This is not something that can be dealt with by an organization or church on its own. Your first responsibility is to protect those who are still vulnerable.

Time factor
In some situations regarding criminal cases, and in many organizations' or professions' own procedures (for example the Anglican Church's new

Clergy Discipline Measure),[7] there is a restricted time limit from when the abuse has taken place, within which complaints can be heard. While accepting that this means evidence is fresher and therefore easier to process, this does discriminate against the victim in abuse cases particularly. We have seen that the dynamics of abuse can be internalized by the victims to such an extent that they do not recognize they were being abused until years later, or they may have held the conscious memory of the abuse, but not have felt strong enough to talk about it. This conspires in many cases with the abuser's attempts to ensure silence, and effectively gags the victim. Abuse procedures should recognize these particular dynamics and remove any statute of limitations, ensuring all abuse allegations are considered carefully whatever the timescale involved.

Speaking out

If you have been abused and are considering reporting, I hope this chapter has not been too depressing. The important thing is that you decide for yourself what is the right thing for you, and at the right time. Unless there are children still at risk and other people who are aware of this (in which case they have a responsibility to act to protect the vulnerable) you do not have to report at all. Maybe it is so long ago you can't remember enough. Maybe you aren't strong enough yet. Maybe you need more time to think about what you hope to achieve. Reporting is a huge and scary step and I cannot pretend it is ever easy. But it can also be empowering, protecting of others, and a positive step towards justice. There are many survivors' books that have more space to advise on this topic (see Chapter 10). I just want to highlight some of the curses and blessings of reporting.

Curses and blessings of reporting

First, the dangers. It is really important to have worked through clearly with a good enlightened witness why you want to report and what you hope to gain from it. It is too easy to raise false hope that our abuser will admit everything and apologize – and everything will be better. It is rarely that perfect. We have to be prepared to be disappointed, denied, sometimes threatened or re-abused; in other words it is important to be feeling brave and to adopt a realistic approach! On the positive side, whether or not there is any personal progress with the abuser, there are still many gains: any report can encourage other survivors to speak out, prevent other abuses and teach the agency concerned to take cases seriously. On a personal level, there is the possibility of further resolution of the unfinished business surrounding the abuse. In the best situations, there is significant healing and reconciliation. The truth is liberated, heard, understood and replaces the abuse as the basis of relationships in the community. The survivor's voice is released at last.

Proclamation

'What we have come to know we must remember, and what we remember we must *tell*' (Volf, 1996, p. 235). Our justice is one that is proclaimed just as the passion is proclaimed each time we share communion. It is proclaimed because that is the nature of justice. And in the proclaiming, good practice can be a beacon of light in the murky waters of abuse and protection. In an age of litigation and compensation, the Church could provide an alternative model that is more concerned with restoring right relationships than self-preservation or material gain. When I attempted to report the clergy person who abused me, I struggled to deal with a system that seemed to me to focus on the latter. What I really wanted and needed was to recover my voice; to have my story heard, to be believed, to be reassured that my abuser was no longer a threat to anyone else and to be supported through the trauma of reporting and the long healing journey that followed. Later, with God's grace, I might wish to effect reconciliation or at least find some way for each party to let go of the past. It may not be possible to restore a trans-formed relationship directly with an abuser, nor do I think it is necessary to do so. The goal is simply for everyone to be able to move on; the original destination may never be revisited. But it is important that both abuser and survivor are supported to face the truth and deal with its implications – in effect each party has to restore their relationship with their community. Both will have issues with the community as well as with each other and themselves; both will feel on the edge, cut off from the community and God, and will need leading back into a right rela-tionship. This is considered further in Chapters 5 and 6.

DISCUSSION QUESTIONS

To discuss
Have you any experience of reporting abuse? Do you agree that the path to truth needs to maintain a balance between care and justice? How well do you see this being achieved in the organizations that you belong to? What happens in them, if someone reports bullying or any kind of abuse?

To reflect
While the adult strives for justice, the voice of the child often longs for sanctuary. How do you imagine God responding to the child? Where are the places of sanctuary and healing in our communities?

To do
To date the experience of people reporting abuse has not all been positive, whether whistle-blowing or disclosures of historic incidents. Is advocacy the best way to ensure the perspective of the survivor is taken into account? What can you do to contribute to good practice in your agency or community?

Notes

1 See Chapter 10 for sources of complaints and disciplinary procedures; Appendix 3 for a sample procedure adaptable to any abuse by adults in an organization; and Appendix 4 for a set of areas to consider when creating good practice procedures for dealing with disclosures of abuse. Full policies are too lengthy to reproduce here; for source materials and organizations, see Chapter 10.

2 Unpublished account, 2002, quoted with permission. Name changed to protect anonymity and for legal reasons.

3 For example, a foster-child may make an allegation against someone in the foster-home when in reality it is the parental home where the abuse is taking place.

4 Adapted from Eric Ludlow, a member of the Social Fund Commissioner's Business Team, <http://www.irs-review.org.uk/infocent/journals/htmljourn/issue12/jrnl12_htm>.

5 Overview précised from original work (unpublished) by Concetta Perot, for Greenbelt 2002 seminar on good practice.

6 Not only did Victoria Climbié's church fail to recognize her abuse despite many obvious signs, instead it was interpreted as demonic and she was subjected to deliverance ministry.

7 The Clergy Discipline Measure for the Church of England received royal assent in July 2003, and is being brought into force gradually over the next two years. See <http://cofe.anglican.org/legal> for the text.

References

Benyei, C., *Understanding Clergy Misconduct in Religious Systems: scapegoating, family secrets and the abuse of power*, Haworth Pastoral Press, New York, 1998.

Chevous, Jane, 'Breaking the Silence', *Third Way*, Vol. 26 No. 1, January/February 2003.

Children's Bill, Bill 144, HMSO, London, 2004.

Gosney, Jeanette, *Surviving Child Sexual Abuse: Supporting Adults in the Church*, Grove Books, Cambridge, 2002.

Every Child Matters, DFES, London, 2003.

Henderson, C., 2002, <http://www.pip.com.au/~chenderson/ggarticl.htm>.

Ludlow, Eric, <http://www/irs-review.org.uk/infocent/journals/htm/journ/issue12/jrnl12_1.htm>.

McFadyen, A., *Bound to Sin: Abuse, Holocaust and the Christian Doctrine of Sin*, Cambridge University Press, Cambridge, 2000.

National Family Mediation, found on <http://www.nfm.u-net.com/menu.htm> accessed January 2004.

Volf, M., *Exclusion and Embrace: A theological exploration of identity, otherness and reconciliation*, Abingdon, Nashville, TN, 1996.

Working Together to Safeguard Children: A guide to interagency working to safeguard and promote the welfare of children, HMSO, London, 1999.

5

The Long Haul:
supporting survivors

————◄○►————

At dawn [Jesus] appeared again in the temple courts, where all the
people gathered round him, and he sat down to teach them. The
teachers of the law brought in a woman caught in adultery. They made
her stand before the group and said to Jesus, 'Teacher, this woman was
caught in the act of adultery. In the Law Moses commanded us to stone
such women. Now what do you say?' . . . But Jesus bent down and
started to write on the ground with his finger. When they kept on
questioning him, he straightened up and said to them, '[Let] any one of
you [who] is without sin, . . . be the first to throw a stone at her.'

John 8.2–7

Margaret Kennedy talked about not looking for the quick fix but
staying around for the long haul.[1] For example, I was first abused over
30 years ago and have spent the last 5 years working through the legacy
in regular counselling. I am not yet at the point where I would call
myself healed, although there has been significant progress. This chapter
talks about the healing journey; the stages on the way and the companions needed. There are indeed passages in 'the valley of the shadow of
death'; but ultimately a hopeful picture emerges of a resurrection
experience from victim to survivor to thriver.

Cairns for the journey

The healing process is often likened to a journey, to emphasize that for
most of us, healing from abuse is a process (like bereavement) rather
than a one-off event. There are a number of publications that function
as a manual for survivors and their counsellors and companions on that
journey (see resources featured in Chapter 10). Here are some glimpses
of the passage in all its painful reality, to assist pilgrims and companions
alike to be prepared for the best and worst of what lies ahead.

Denial

Abuse is not something a victim can make sense of. There is no obvious reason if we are truthful and logical, why my father/priest/sister/partner should treat me in this way. He may say I want it and it's a special treat; but I know deep down that it is ugly, painful and wrong. I may be told it is my fault and I deserve it; but somewhere in my soul there is a child that recognizes the mendacity of these tales. It's like a robot in panic mode: it does not compute. What I am told and experience, what I feel and reality do not add up. So survivors adopt coping strategies to deal with this irresolvable conflict; and one of the easiest is denial. It didn't happen to me, I had a lovely childhood, she was a good person. Minimization often follows; it wasn't that bad, it didn't do me any harm, it only happened for a few years.

The very first step is to acknowledge the truth and thus release the story of the abuse. Gradually in the re-telling the experience is re-examined in a more realistic and balanced framework and the true impact and responsibility assessed.

Depression

Someone once described the root of depression as anger turned inwards, and I still consider that definition contains a simple truth. There are more complex physiological conditions such as manic depression. Here I am dealing with the all-too-common state of depressive illness. Abuse is in essence about a powerless state, and the inability to express anger towards the real culprit is enough to plunge anyone into the depths of despair. The trouble with depression is that the feelings can be so overwhelming that it is hard to find the energy or motivation to change the situation. Depression is sitting at the bottom of a dark, deep well of pain without even the energy to lift your head to see the light or to lift your hand to grasp the rope. Sometimes the only way to help is to climb down to the bottom with the sufferer and gently nurture back the flicker of life. Not to rescue – we all need to learn to keep our own life-flame fed.

Depression at its most dangerous becomes suicidal, as death seems the easiest, least painful, or only option. We are too drawn into our pain to be able to see enough of the bigger picture, to realize there is a better choice. Helpers need to provide glimpses of that more hopeful picture; and to hold on to the stark truth that we can only ever be responsible for our own life, not another's. Depression is more than sadness; it is the bleak isolation of Psalm 13:

> How long, O Lord? Will you forget me for ever?
> How long will you hide your face from me?
> How long must I wrestle with my thoughts
> And every day have sorrow in my heart?
> How long will my enemy triumph over me?

Friends and family can help by breaking into the isolation with companionship and a listening ear; and encouraging the expression of the
deep emotions within a safe environment. Tears and rage are a great
release.

Anger

Christians too often are afraid of anger, or condemn it disapprovingly.
Yet righteous anger at injustice is a key theological theme and explicitly
modelled by Jesus. For survivors who have been taught or shaped to
turn anger in on themselves instead of towards their abusers, connecting with a righteous anger and finding safe ways to express it back
outwards where it belongs can be a powerful key that unlocks another
gate to the path to healing. In fact the most important Christian stance
could be to offer support and encouragement to express anger, rather
than discouragement. To be angry about what has been done to me, I
first have to believe that I matter enough not to have deserved it, and to
understand that it was not my fault. This is where other survivors can
be key – as I discover my anger on their behalf, I learn the possibility of
feeling the same for myself.

Being able to express anger safely and appropriately is important.
There may be abuse victims who pose a danger to others but those I
have met only ever threaten themselves (self-harm can be one manifes-
tation of this). Communities can express anger on behalf of all victims
through worship, acts of witness or art, for example. This is supportive
and affirming to victims and gives both permission and an appropriate
space to express personal frustration, rage and even desire for revenge.
Enactments – smashing plates, bashing cardboard boxes or hitting
pillows – undertaken with good and careful support become therapeutic rituals that release some of the pent-up rage and pain we carry. It is
like lancing a boil; we need to get the gunge out to clean the wound and
allow the space for healing. Imaginary revenge can be a way of gaining
the satisfaction without all the hassles and implications of the real thing!
Psalms (and other gory bits of the Bible) again are useful here. Even
Jesus pronounced to the Pharisees: 'upon you will come all the righteous
blood that has been shed on earth' (Matthew 23.35a) – a gory justice
indeed.

Shame and joy

'Where there is no shame there is no honour.'[2] There is hope in this
truism if one can dare to take the reverse as true: it is because I still have
honour (in myself) that I feel so ashamed. It is a normal experience for
survivors of all types of abuse to take on the burden of the perpetrator's
sinful actions, and to feel totally ashamed of themselves and the events
they have been part of. It feeds the belief of worthlessness and the
diminished sense of self, referred to in Chapter 2. It can be based on an

understanding of culpability for the sin that has happened, which is transferred into the idea that I am sinful.

The restoration of responsibility where it belongs (see Chapter 3) should help to remove this misplaced culpability and the stain of sin. That it is not so easy reflects the powerful conditioning affecting the survivor's worldview and the distorted image she sees projected from the looking-glass. Gosney (2002) suggests we can restore our 'shattered identity' through seeing mirrored in the eyes of God and of others, our essential goodness as God's beloved. Gradually, she suggests, we recognize in the Christ-child our own damaged inner child and learn within the Christ-encounter to love and be loved again, 'to re-member' who we are.

I see this restoration of self-honouring as something akin to restoring the capacity for joy in relation to oneself, others, the world and God as described by McFadyen (2000, p. 238). Abuse, he suggests, is the distortion 'in theological terms, of worship – of the possibility of standing in the proper economy of thanks and praise of God, which requires dynamic self-affirmation and openness to others in loving joy'. This image has all the richness of the feasting and flourishing of Ford's 'articulated essay' on salvation (Ford, 1999).

Relinquishment and reshaping

Nydam (2002) talking about adoption, identifies the importance of understanding its duality: 'relinquishment and adoption are separate, although parallel, lifelong processes that influence and impact each other in a variety of ways'. I am also adopted, and this idea brought enlightenment to my adoptee identity and resonated strongly with the survivor experience. The experience of abuse creates many losses to mourn: a childhood, a marriage, perhaps a church and always the potential of a healthy relationship. There is also the personal loss of safety, identity, worth and trust. One therapeutic concept identifies the 'inner child' as the part of us frozen in the time of the abuse, trapped by the feelings and conditioned responses of that experience and still reacting to triggering situations as though we were still there. It can be seen as the dynamic of abuse integrated into our very identity that McFadyen describes when exploring original sin (McFadyen, 2000). Survivors have talked about grieving for the lost child and some have even enacted a symbolic funeral, acknowledging that for them it is as if a part of them did not survive.

I have found it helpful to recognize this relinquishment – whatever it means to me – as a drawn-out process not a single act. It is part of the letting go of the memory of the abuse, the damage it has caused, the consequences for myself and those I love, and all the 'might-have-beens' that form my regrets. It can be like a stripping away, removing layers as in the powerful image from Narnia of Eustace scraping off his dragon scales.[3] I believe the most important relinquishment is the adapted self that the abuser has created. The act of changing the script of my conditioning restores me to the wholeness that was the intention of my creator.

I don't mean by this that I have to wipe out or forget the shape of my identity that has been formed through the abuse. It is as much a part of me as any other and it would not be healthy to repeat the denial that characterizes the victim place. Rather I envisage an embracing of my identity that transforms it and enables me to transcend the lowest place of my worthlessness. It is the eschatological orientation of suffering transformed by hope that Moltmann writes about so passionately.[4] In the twentieth century, a similar reclaiming can be seen in the women's movement, Black Pride, and in the disability equality movement's rejection of 'impairment' as a state of deficiency. I am who I am. For some survivors, it is symbolized by the embracing of the vulnerable inner child who we denied, neglected or even hated for so long.

Health is restored through this positive act of regeneration. Sometimes this renewal of identity can be described by the Christian and therapeutic communities as though it requires the destruction of the old me and the creation of a new model – mark two, vastly improved! There is an uncomfortable duality behind this understanding that I struggle with, theologically. It is God as destructive eraser instead of creative pen. Rather I understand it as a reshaping. My essence doesn't change – I am still the person who has been squashed into a victim shape, distorted and crushed. I don't adopt a new form in the sense of taking one from outside of myself. Gradually at times, at others in accelerated bursts, I break out of the prison of abuse and reform into something that approaches more the shape of the one in whose image I was first formed. Like the resurrected Jesus, I still bear the scars but the wounds are healed. Through reshaping I am restored.

Stumbling blocks

A journey from 'dis-ease' to health is often a challenging one, and for survivors there are many traps and obstacles to face. It appears to me quite significant to our understanding of abuse and its effects that the same themes appear again and again in survivors' stories. We have looked at depression, and considered how anger can be a positive force for justice. Here some other areas are examined that have limited benefit and may even sabotage growth and the regaining of health.

Self-harm and body theology
'Being a self-harmer is a big taboo anyway, but admitting it to a group of Christians?! Instead of support and compassion, I have faced judgement and isolation from group settings. There seems to be a

tendency to see the action as wrong and detach that from the vulnerable person behind the action.'[5]

My experience in survivors' networks is that self-injury, alcohol and drug misuse and eating disorders are common issues that we struggle with. In some Christian circles there is a damaging judgemental attitude to this, which I hope may be lessened by a greater understanding. In Chapter 9 I explore some theological issues of the body and try to use these to cast some further light on the issues and experiences of self-harming.

Misusing drugs and alcohol in response to the major trauma of abuse can be seen, like eating disorders and self-injury, as both an expression of suffering and a coping strategy for the past and present realities. There is contention about the extent to which the latter are also addictive behaviours that require a medical intervention. The over-whelming evidence from survivors, backed up by the latest research,[6] demonstrates that the real issues are about identity and context rather than any physical condition.

Until recently, I don't believe we have paid enough attention to understanding the different self-harming strategies adopted by many abuse survivors. In the Church there is a danger we have viewed them as sins, and responded with judgement, when careful analysis reveals they are adapted behaviours signalling the need for support to deal with underlying issues. There are some good publications and projects now appearing that inform on each of the examples I have mentioned (see Chapter 10). I will focus on just one example in more depth, in order to dispel common myths and relate some of the complex dynamics involved.

The popular image of self-harm is that it is:

- an addiction (e.g. drug mis-use)
- controlling (e.g. eating disorders)
- attention-seeking (e.g. cutting)
- a deliberate choice (i.e. indicating irrationality)
- suicidal (i.e. stemming from hopelessness)

Focusing on self-injury as an example, I want to refute all of these myths. A leading expert on self-mutilation, Armando Favazza, defines it as 'the deliberate, direct, nonsuicidal destruction or alteration of one's body tissue' (in Strong 2000, p. x). He classifies it into three types; the least severe of these – 'moderate/superficial mutilation' – is what I refer to here and is most common among survivors. Most common methods are cutting with razors, knives, broken glass or similar sharp objects, or burning (e.g. with cigarettes); other behaviours include picking, hair-pulling, hitting things with different parts of the body and jumping from great heights.

There is growing understanding of the chemical and hormonal reactions in the body that are associated with trauma and self-injury. This has been used as evidence that it is an addiction. However, what has been discovered is that reminders of major trauma trigger the body to produce natural pain–relievers and stress hormones. It is unclear exactly what relationship this has to cutting. Does the numbness of the body-response induce dissociation – and cutting is a way to feel again? Or is it the withdrawal from the natural chemicals the body produces – which are narcotics – that creates an addiction? The cutting may be induced by the high anxiety and hyper arousal of the stress hormones. These issues can be helpful in identifying appropriate treatment. But they do not help us to understand the underlying reasons for starting to self-injure.

In fact the opposite of the five popular myths is true:

- The starting point is not addiction but trauma and lack of self-worth – for many it is abusive episodes in childhood and a perception that one's life has no value.
- It is the sign of a person out of control: for survivors, the perpetrator was in charge not them; the buried history and trauma are in control of life now. Self-injury is a way of trying to wrest some control back, but it quickly becomes another area which is closer to self-destruction than order.
- It is not a choice in that there are no other realistic options. Self-harmers cut out of desperation, hopelessness, overwhelming emotions such as pain, fear or anger. They cut to deal with an intolerable situation that they cannot see another way out of.
- It is nevertheless a hopeful activity. It is not simply a step towards suicide, although self-harmers may also be depressed and may attempt suicide as well. Cutting is an attempt to cope with the trauma of the abuse and can be seen as suicide-prevention or avoidance.
- It is not an aggressive activity. Cutters have been characterized as dangerous to others but this is rarely the case. It is the self that is the target of the activity, because the need is to deal with pain not to cause it; and there can be a deliberate choice to hurt oneself out of fear that buried anger about the abuse, for example, may otherwise be directed at others.

All the different kinds of self-harm mentioned, seen in this framework, can be recognized as a symptom of the underlying disease rather than the root problem. However, they can also become a substitute for healthy strategies and hinder the survivor's progress. Once there is some mending of the underlying wound, it is important to find the right exercises to build up strength and not become reliant on the crutch that has been so important for initial survival. An essential tool during crisis and in the initial stages of recovery, the danger of becoming too reliant is that there is never a time when we can walk and run again unsupported.

Specialist agencies are particularly helpful in understanding and supporting survivors who are wrestling with self-injury, eating disorders, drug or alcohol dependency and other harmful strategies. Key agencies and resources are highlighted in Chapter 10. Survivors, friends and supporters can also help in many uncomplicated ways to find more creative and life-affirming aids to recovery. These range from immediate danger substitutes (such as drawing with red pens rather than cutting) to simple restorative tools (such as a pampering bath with candles and perfumed bubbles). See Appendix 5 for further suggestions.

Hiding and revelation

If we understand the destination of our healing pilgrimage to be the restoration of joyfulness, it becomes clear that hiding from the abuse and its consequences is another survival strategy that has drawbacks as well as benefits. There are many different kinds of hiding that survivors can adopt, all of which may offer necessary protection at particular times. Through dissociation I may hide from the abuse while it is taking place and from its memory. I may bury the knowledge of the abuse and the feelings it created deep in an inaccessible part of my being. I may physically run away and hide. I may hide from other people, avoiding contact, involvement, and commitment. I am likely to hide from myself and from God.

It is good to create a place of safety, while the abuse is still happening, to protect from risk of further abuse and to provide a space for healing. The trouble is that while I am protected from the abuse, I am also isolated from good and loving relationships. While I keep other people at arm's length, I risk no pain but deflect warmth and nourishment as well. Hiding is an instinct of shame as well as fear: 'I was afraid because I was naked; so I hid' (Genesis 3.10b). I cover myself to avoid exposure of my vulnerability and because I am ashamed of who I am. A healing path is one that nurtures a careful process of revelation, helping me to have the courage and strength to accept myself as I am and show my true self to the world.

The total knowledge God has of me is both frightening and awesome. Psalm 139 summarizes these mixed feelings perfectly; it is both disconcerting (to one ashamed) that 'you have searched me and you know me', and wonderful (to one longing for love) that 'you created my innermost being; you knit me together in my mother's womb'. One of the other difficulties with such total knowing is the possibility that I have been created for the abuse; it is more comfortable for my fate to remain unknown to God than to understand predestination to mean that God knew what would happen to me and at best chose not to prevent it, at worst meant it to be so. Hiding protects me from this possible conclusion and maintains my faith in a God who is good and desires only the best for me. The theological pitfalls around this are discussed further in Chapter 9. The point is that unless I can reveal myself to God in all my broken humanity, I cannot fully experience her loving embrace. Hearing the Song of Songs as a celebration of God's relationship with us, here is the most beautiful of intimacy, the deepest joy, which is the blessing waiting for us when we are free from the captivity of concealment.

Forced forgiveness

> Forgiving an abuser can never be straightforward and no-one can understand unless they've been there. That's not a judgemental thing; it is just that it is a big thing to get your head around.
>
> Forgiveness should come out of love, and you can only love them when you've made the time and given yourself permission to look at the tough stuff.[7]

I have lost count of the number of survivors who report having been told by Christians that they should forgive their abuser. This may be well meaning, but is dangerously simplistic, ill-informed and frequently re-abusive. In the worst stories, there is pressure to forgive indecently soon after the disclosure of abuse; injunctions to forgive and forget; a directive that reporting the abuse to the police is not a suitably Christian action; the judgement that reluctance to forgive and 'just hand it over to God' is unchristian and the cause of unhealth; counsel to reconcile with the abuser as an act of forgiveness.

The nature of forgiveness and an appropriate theology is explored further in Chapter 9. Here I want to deal briefly with some of the other issues raises by the examples above.

The 'no cheap fixes' injunction applies as much to forgiveness as to any part of the complex process of dealing with the aftermath of abuse. If we understand forgiveness as a process, not a single act of will, it should be obvious that it takes time to complete. It is similar to the stages of the bereavement journey, and equally unpredictable in the length of time it may take. Nobody would counsel a recent widow to hasten to forget and move on; neither is it appropriate or reasonable to rush a survivor. Furthermore, forgiveness is part of the connected process of reconciliation and restoration, touched upon in Chapter 3. Without recognition, repentance and reparation from the abuser, it is unreasonable to demand that the victim unilaterally forgives. Even with these (sadly uncommon) preparations, it is hard to let go and set all parties free. Only the grace of God can bring us to the point of saying 'it is finished'.

The misconception that reporting an offender is unchristian brings us into very dubious territory. Not only does it fly against our national legal framework, all recognized good practice and most church and organizational policies and procedures, it also ignores the welfare of the offender and the whole community as much as that of the victim. God may love us unconditionally but we are expected to take responsibility for our actions, even if the consequences are much less punitive than we deserve. An offence not investigated is a truth buried; an offence unreported is an offender left in sin, a community left without due process of justice and a victim abandoned to deal with the consequences alone.

Reluctance by a survivor to forgive hastily is a very healthy place to be. The process of reaching forgiveness, while clearly desirable, is a complex dance that requires some practice. It involves difficult steps such as facing the truth of what has occurred, moving away from shameful denial and reclaiming one's value as worthy of restoration, dealing with anger, pain, distrust and all the legacies of the abuse. Enforced forgiveness is untruthful, unprepared, rootless and potentially damaging and transient; it is unlikely to lead to health and wholeness. Better to be a partner, sometimes leading, sometimes following, but letting the survivor choose the dance and set the pace.

Reconciliation with the abuser is a very delicate and potentially explosive area. The definitive paradigm of the crucifixion is that ultimately only God can bring about true reconciliation. There are so many issues to address before even considering this option. Has the abuser acknowledged and repented the abuse? Is the victim strong enough and far enough along her healing journey? Who else in the immediate family and surrounding community need to be taken into account? Would the victim be exposed to the danger of further abuse? Who is available to witness and mediate? What is the appropriate method of communication – does there need to be a face-to-face meeting? If there is a criminal or other investigation under way, will reconciliation contaminate the evidence or prejudice a fair trial?

While biblical teaching on the importance of forgiveness is clear, there is nothing to suggest that this always has to result in interpersonal reconciliation. Neither is there a guarantee that offering the olive branch will necessarily be successful in re-establishing a broken relationship. We are asked to restore our unity with our brother or sister before coming to the altar; but the difficulty of forgiving an enemy is acknowledged and not linked with reconciliation. Jesus did not exactly adopt a conciliatory approach to the religious authorities of the time, whom one might argue were his clearest enemies by virtue of their role in bringing about his crucifixion. Indeed, it would not exactly be exaggerating to say he seemed to take some delight in provoking them, and indulged in a full-blown rant against the teachers of the law and the

Pharisees on one particularly memorable occasion (Matthew 23.1–36). It was an act of shalom, in community, that brought about reconciliation to God; and this model of collective rather than individual responsibility provides a better model for our efforts to restore relationships without the misplacing of trust. The cracks that abuse opens within families and communities may take several generations and many different players to fill or bridge.

A communion of pilgrims

Companion

Companions are always needed on the healing journey. There are many times when an abuse victim might choose to be alone or feel safer alone and may even reject friendship offered. Like a hurt animal, the fight or flight response is strong. Abuse, however, is ultimately about betrayal of trust and broken relationships; yet as children of God we are made in and for relationship. Learning to trust and receive support again is a vital part of the process. The word 'companion' comes from the Latin *com panis* and literally means one who shares bread with another. The rich overtones of this image illustrate the best of healing journeys, a communion with each other, each of us sharing the essentials of life and the essence of God.

Safe and understanding companions are hard to find. The idea of the 'enlightened witness'[8] – one who hears, sees the abuse (re-told) and understands the truth of what they observe – brings the notion of companionship to a sharper focus. A variety of roles can be important at different times and obviously individuals will differ in what they need and what helps. Only the Archangel Gabriel should attempt them all! Sometimes supporting a survivor can seem an overwhelming task and companions fear they are ill equipped or inadequate for the challenges the journey brings. It is good to focus on the role that best reflects your particular qualities and gifts; it is my experience that God provides by making sure you are in the right place at the right time. (See Appendix 6 for guidelines on best practice on supporting survivors.)

Listener

Hearing the story of the abuse is the single most important and liberating act anyone can undertake. It is not about pitying the person who has been abused, nor parenting them, simply listening and reflecting your honest reaction to what you hear. It is important to accept with openness what you are hearing; the veiled disbelief in phrases such as 'Are you sure . . . ?' could easily stop dead the first tentative words of disclosure. Many survivors expect to be disbelieved and indeed have come a long way in order to trust themselves enough to tell their story at all; abusers commonly convince their victims that no one will believe them if they try to disclose. The power of the story comes in its affirmation of my experience. It breaks the prison of secrecy. It gives expression to the survivor's voice.

The normal tools of good listening apply in this situation too. It helps to create a safe and confidential environment, not to be frightened of silences or pauses, and to allow the process to happen at an unhurried pace. It is particularly important not to succumb to the danger of bringing in your own issues. It is not your story and your view and experiences are not relevant here. It is good to affirm the real feelings and thoughts that the story prompts in you; telling a weighty story to a deadpan listener is a very unnerving experience! But the real focus of your attention should remain on the storyteller, and your energy is best spent giving gentle encouragement for the tale to emerge in its own way. To me, the heart of listening lies in absorbing the picture being woven before you and empathizing with the narrator, a silent witness standing (or sitting or crouching) beside them. No further intervention is required at this stage. Being heard is the most enormous first step and is far enough to go for many survivors for a long time. It breaks the silence.

Accompanist

> Trauma is about separation from the people or beliefs that protect, nurture and guide us . . .
>
> Recovery is all about creating attachment in a person's life. It's about the relief of suffering. (Elia Vecchione[9])

The term 'accompanying' is used here with a recent emphasis that describes a timeless activity. It is the joy and struggle of walking alongside another person through thick and thin, scaling the heights and plunging the depths of life from their perspective. It is the incarnational role of living with them in the darkness and the pain, in order to assist their coming into the light. It is 'being there' in the fullest sense we can imagine the term to mean. The best of friends do this. Partners can be helpful accompanists but they also have another role, which is more involved and is essentially reciprocal. Accompanying is not offered on the basis of expecting a return; the soloist has the tune.

> This is accompanying, providing a framework, a safe base which the accompanied can use to explore different themes in their lives. A good accompanist is sensitive, attentive and knows that the creative energy to explore these themes comes from the accompanied themselves. An accompanist listens and is alert to those themes which are hidden and obscured and gently provides a framework and space where the accompanied can reveal and explore these for their growth and development. (Green and Christian, 1998, p. 20)

Green and Christian suggest that the best qualities of an accompanist arise from a calling rather than any training or practice. They point to qualities such as empathy, tolerance, wisdom and grace and mark the importance of the accompanist being grounded and secure enough in their own life and being so as not to be unduly undermined or thrown off course by whatever emerges from the person being accompanied. Someone in crisis is not normally well equipped to support another in crisis, but this is not to overstate the case. An accompanist retains their human frailties as well as strengths, learning and growing with the one accompanied. It can be in sharing *our* vulnerability that we best enable a survivor to accept the gift of *hers*, and nurture the reshaping from victim to thriver.

Of course the total 'knowing' of a close friend can also be scary; as with our nakedness before God, our cry might be 'where can I flee from your presence?' (Psalm 139). A survivor's own lack of self-worth accentuates the fear: I don't want you to know my worthlessness, I am ashamed of what I have revealed to you, I may mistrust what you will do with the insights we have shared. To create the relationship of trust that is fundamental to developing good accompanying, it is important to face these fears openly and explore what may bring safety or prove them unfounded.

How close should this accompanying relationship be? In a recent sermon series on Ruth and Naomi, entitled 'Reclaiming the bitter years', my vicar pointed out how the Bible passage describes Ruth as *clinging* to Naomi when she was about to leave. He suggested that we all need someone to cling to, especially through troubled times.[10] The old word is 'cleave', which is also used to describe the marital relationship. I am not suggesting that only married partners can be accompanists! But perhaps that quality of attachment is an important one, especially for survivors who struggle to trust binding relationships (see Chapter 2). There is much healing in the union itself; the experience of recognizing that the abuser is *not* bound to me for ever, but a true friend (like God) will never let me go.

Advocate

I was surprised to discover that research indicates that 40–60 per cent of people experiencing domestic violence will tell someone, at least a friend, about their situation; surprised partly because telling is such a hard step to take, but also because research also suggests that less than 60 per cent of situations are dealt with by the authorities. That means a lot of friends know about the dangers but may not have been willing or able to intervene to improve the situation. An obvious conclusion is that strong advocates, who are prepared to act on what they have heard, would make a real difference to the prevalence of abuse in our communities.

The boundary around the role of advocate is an important one. An advocate supports victims to make their own interventions; and speaks out for them when their voices are unheard or silenced. An advocate has the interests of their friend (or client) at heart and fights for their corner. They intervene only where the victim is unable to do so for themselves (perhaps through age, or ability to cope with official processes at a vulnerable time). They speak not with their own voice but with their friend's and refer all possible decisions back to them.

Another important advocacy role is in fighting for the support and resources needed to deal with abuse and its aftermath. Here, Christian and caring organizations could take a much more leading role in campaigning for more resources to be channelled into training and therapy, in particular. Education that raises awareness of all the issues laid out here among both professionals and the whole community, must also have the potential to contribute to a less abusive society. Awareness can be raised within the Church through sermons and themed acts of worship (see resources section in Chapter 10 for some ideas); we need to provide the best opportunities we can for the Spirit to enlighten and transform us! A community conference that brought together leaders, agencies dealing with abuse, and survivors and their families and supporters would enable both networking and learning to take place. There are not many opportunities for survivors to communicate their feelings and perspectives to the professionals involved in protection and response, outside of intervention and treatment. Christian organizations could initiate and host such encounters as well as benefiting from participating.

Self-help group
Although at first another big and scary step, many survivors find talking with other survivors very powerful and an effective support to healing. They are more 'enlightened witnesses' than most; they rarely judge or condemn, understand without difficult explanations; and affirm identity and experience through the echoes and reflections that are their own. They are empathetic accompanists and skilled peer mentors: for example, the co-accountability and positive encouragement of a self-harm forum. They also don't let you get away unchallenged with unhealthy coping strategies that others often miss: dissociation, masking, denial and self-denial, self-harm.

There are disadvantages to self-help groups (which to my mind don't outweigh the benefits). Although not borne out in my experience, it has been suggested that a group with one or two influential members in a very negative place can drag the rest down; certainly they can be painful places to be and we have to take responsibility for withdrawing if we need to, in order to keep ourselves safe. Second, like any significant issue, if we spend all or most of our time within the world of abuse, it can skew our perspective of life. It is important to inhabit spaces where being a survivor is not the most significant thing about us and where abuse is not the main focus of interactions.

Running a self-help group is both empowering and energy-draining for members, who are after all already coping with a lot of demands. Churches and caring organizations can help to provide encouragement, premises and publicity for a fledgling group. See Chapter 10 for details of a newly launched Christian network.

Counsellor/therapist

Many survivors of abuse find a therapist or counsellor a key source of support and help during their healing journey. However well provided you are with committed family and friends (and many of us are not), there are some areas that need informed assistance; some agendas we may not be ready to share with them; some demands that tip the balance of give and take in our committed relationships just too far. It can also be helpful to create a separate, safe space where some of the hard work of revealing and reshaping can happen, freeing up time with the family as space just to get on with life. It helps survivors not to be defined by the abuse.

Perhaps the key role of a therapist is that of enlightened witness; someone who understands the story beneath the story, who can teach you to interpret what happened and re-frame it from the perspective of a survivor not a victim. The confused thinking that abuse creates can be sorted out here; a counsellor can help you to recognize what belongs to you and what does not, from the muddle of issues and feelings carried around as the legacy of abuse. Another positive aspect of the therapist as witness is the fact that someone else has heard us, beyond our immediate circle. In a sense they can then represent the wider community, another important aspect of breaking the silence.

The variety of different approaches to therapy will suit different people. It is important to research what is available, consider what suits you and test the ground carefully. Within the different approaches, perhaps the most fundamental issue to consider is: who is in charge of the healing process, client or therapist? Particularly in the context of recovering from abuse, I think there are some issues with a therapist who wants to direct the process, not least because it mirrors the 'I know better than you what's good for you' attitude played by many abusers.

In my experience the person-centred approach is the most empowering; the survivor takes back control of his or her life and seeks his own solutions. Guidance, experience, new perspectives from another can all be helpful if offered, not imposed. An agreed level of accountability can accompany non-judgemental acceptance by the counsellor; for example, it can help to break out of the habit of self-harming if I have someone safe to whom I can report my successes and admit any slips.

Therapy has been criticized for being self-indulgent, encouraging 'false memories' and leaving people stuck in the negativity of a victim place. I can only say that this appears true of a minority of incompetent and untrained therapists! There is no credible research to substantiate the 'false memories' claim for competent and well-supervised therapy. I cannot see how going to a counsellor to address emotional, spiritual and mental ill-health is any more self-indulgent than going to a medical doctor with a broken leg. There is no shortage of evidence from people who have gained very positive outcomes from a period of counselling; and some evidence to suggest that those who remain stuck, maybe left before enough work was done to sustain the benefits, rather like stopping taking antibiotics mid-course, when the first effects are felt. In fact the only disadvantages I can see are that it's difficult to find a good counsellor when you need one, and most people (of all ages) have to pay for it themselves, which for an individual of average means is a big financial commitment, and for anyone of limited means, virtually impossible.

I have been privileged to share my journey with a Christian counsellor who is both person-centred and totally involved, without the element of detachment that some practitioners espouse. She embodies the understanding of the enlightened witness, the commitment and empowerment of the accompanist, the solidarity of the advocate and the safety of sanctuary. In the womb-space she creates, I have learnt to reveal all and trust that I can be safe. I have been able to bring my needs and know they are acceptable; if I want to spend my hour in silence, cuddled in her arms, they are opened. If I need to disgorge my anger, there are cushions to beat and a tennis racket to hit them with. If I am ready to stutter out my story, there is a supportive listener beside me who does not flinch at the messy details. If I am beyond words, there is paper and coloured pens for my child within to draw out her picture-tale. If I am groping towards a new insight, or trapped in the mis-message of the abuser, there is a clear reflection to enable revelation. In all the confused images and feelings of the journey, there is the total comfort of someone who is with me every painful inch of the way. Like being wrapped in the warmest and softest of cloaks, she offers the unconditional and loving acceptance of the incarnation – God in flesh, bringing life and liberation.

Lover

For a while a favourite worship song at our youth service was a Matt Redman chorus, which includes the words 'What a friend I've found, closer than a mother, I can feel your touch, more intimate than lovers . . .' This can be a terrifying image for people who have been abused by those who should have loved them. If the experience of abuse has been from one who should have offered 'good' love – parent or partner or carer – trusting and attaching to a new lover can be very difficult for survivors. The promise of a God who loves is also very frightening. How do we know we can trust God? The stories in the Old Testament are not always reassuring – God appears to do all kinds of violent and angry things. Yet Jesus and Paul talk a lot about love – different kinds of love, not just the safety of agape but the passion and risk of eros. This is not just a big teddy-bear-hug father's love and protection. This is the passionate love and coiled energy of the lioness mother-God, even the sexuality of the Song of Songs, with its richly sensual imagery, innuendo and pounding hearts.

So the intense longing for true love within many survivors is tensioned against flight-instinct fear of further abuse. Only good loving experiences – both platonic and passionate – can begin to remove that barrier. Reluctance overcome, survivors may find that it is the experience of God's love that helps them to trust humans again; and the experience of human love that assists a more wholesome and true understanding of God's love. Re-learning love in reality is most important for those abused as children; it is one thing to know what good love shouldn't be, it is another to be able to offer something you have never felt or received. For those who have experienced sexual abuse, this is a particularly sensitive area. I may have learnt that sex is the currency of love so expect it in any relationship, even offer it – 'take me, I'm nothing'. Or I may find any kind of touch abhorrent. A good lover needs to hold very clear boundaries for me to learn the priceless gift of intimacy; and to wait patiently for me to emerge from my hide of isolation, not demanding anything, before I can offer and receive safe touch again.

Family

Family members may take on some of the roles described above, but may not be able to fulfil all of these, and that is not necessarily a bad thing. It is very helpful for recovery to be more than just a survivor; to have a place where the abuse is not the only or definitive thing about you. The great thing about families that get on with the rest of their lives is that you can be a multi-faceted person and still truly yourself. Sometimes you may all be working on the abuse together; and families can bring the understanding and support that helps to get us through the hardest places. At other times home, sustenance, entertainment, children, finances and other issues will be more important and demand time and energy. It is good that the abuse doesn't dominate our lives (that can be re-abusive). It is good that our needy child within learns that in families she receives nurture, but also has to share. It is of the utmost importance to learn that in sharing, there is always enough love to go round.

Families can be places where we find we can make mistakes and it is not the end of the world. Partners, parents, siblings and children can teach us to receive as well as give; and to give from love not because of fear or conditioning. Families are there through relationship, responsibility and commitment, not just because it is their job, or we have paid them to do it, or they are also survivors, or we are their latest 'good cause'. Sometimes families will also let us down, and the fruits of good healing are evident in our ability to cope with the joys and disappointments caused by human frailty. Survivors may need reminding that families are neither all bad nor all good; the aim is not perfection but 'good enough'.

The legacy of abuse does place enormous strain on family members, especially when the abuse itself happened within the family context. Even if the abuser has moved on or is dead, there may be divisions and mistrust to deal with. If the abuser is still around and perhaps there is some contact, the family has the additional challenge of working out how to deal with that relationship as well. (Some of the issues discussed in Chapter 6 may also be helpful here.) It is just as important for the extended family members to consider their support needs, as it is for the survivor. There are a few organizations that cater for family members and partners of survivors; some are highlighted in Chapter 10. Family members need to develop their ability to discern when the load created by the abuse is too heavy to bear alone and ask for help before reaching crisis stage. This might mean researching information that helps to understand the type of abuse that has taken place and some of the particular issues it is raising. Some family members may have their own personal issues triggered or may have strong emotions raised and find counselling is also helpful for them. A self-help group for families and partners or family therapy may provide a safe space to work through responses to what is looked on as a family unit, not just a collection of individuals. These are all areas where churches and Christian organizations could initiate much-needed support for all family members affected by abuse.

Sanctuary

Abusive relationships are dangerous places. For example, an incidence of domestic violence takes place in the UK every 6–20 seconds. Every 10 seconds someone will be injured. An average of two women a week are killed in domestic violence situations in England and Wales, representing nearly half of all female homicides.

Children have identified some of the most important needs families have once they are in a safe place (ESRC, 2000). These include a secure environment with familiar items if they have left the family home. Somewhere to concentrate on homework was important to some children. A trustworthy confidante and full participation in the decision-making process were important requests not yet often met. Given practical support and the respect of having their opinions listened to and taken seriously, children are durable survivors and have much to teach adult victims and anyone aiming to assist them. Simple clarity is profound; the children wanted 'support, understanding and reassurance, to be in safety with their mothers and to have their own belongings around them' (ESRC, 2000, p. 1).

It is hard to identify many places of sanctuary for survivors of different types of abusive situations. The main refuge network for those fleeing domestic violence is for women and children only and struggles to cope with the demand. It is hard to recruit and retain sufficient and appropriate foster carers to offer children at risk of significant harm a safe family environment if their usual family context cannot provide one. Most people coming forward as adoptive parents want cute babies, not damaged teenagers. Group homes are not the easiest of places to live and work in and may not be able to offer the safe, stable and loving environment each human being needs from their home. Even specialist places offering temporary sanctuary for survivors of any age are rare and very hard to find.

The cost of such provision is normally pointed to as one of the reasons for the scarcity of resources. I don't accept this as a complete justification; after all, it's a question of political priorities whether sanctuary for survivors or new roads or the latest military equipment gets first call on the public purse. There is a community issue here, prompting us all to consider where we want to see public and charitable resources deployed and how to communicate that clearly to decision-makers.

But I don't think we can off-load all responsibility onto the shoulders of public servants. We share responsibility for the abuse in our communities and we need to play an equal role in finding creative and successful responses. There are gaps in two obvious areas of need: immediate places of safety for victims to flee to when safety demands it; and sanctuary in the offering of healing places to support survivors (and those around them, including abusers) through the journey to restoration. One might imagine many different manifestations of this type of sanctuary, from retreat houses to mediation centers, from self-help groups to expert networks, and the models of good practice do exist (see Chapter 10 for a few examples). Often, though, they are inaccessible to most people because of cost or distance; many more local initiatives are needed. It is to local communities that we need to look for places and services that everyone can call on; if churches are at the heart of their neighbourhood, here is another chance to make a real difference, entirely fitting to our call to be a place of refuge and sanctuary for anyone who seeks it.

Community action

There are a few other ways that communities and organizations can take positive action on abuse which are worth a mention here. There is a real need for education and awareness-raising that continues to break the silence for survivors and their supporters, moving beyond the sensationalism of the popular press. Parents, children and young people, community leaders, agencies particularly active in preventing and dealing with abuse and its legacy; all these groups need special training to equip them for their role in prevention and response. But there is an equally important task in raising public awareness generally, and many ways to do so – from an article in a parish magazine to an awareness event at a local library or school. Education is needed not just for recognizing and dealing with abuse, but also for identifying ways to prevent abuse and adopt good practice in leadership and personal and professional relationships.

In many sections of this book I have highlighted the need for more resources and also the political will at all levels of our institutional and community life to address the needs of survivors and everyone affected by abuse. Local policy needs reviewing in this area: there are campaigning organizations to support; and individuals can also make a difference in their particular sphere. For example, someone who works in a school could make their own contribution to implementing an effective child protection policy and providing appropriate resources for survivors and their supporters in both the staff room and the classroom. Someone who works in the health service could campaign for more resources to be channelled into making affordable therapy easily available to survivors (all my GP could offer me was a prescription for Prozac or the phone number of the Samaritans – I rejected the former but did have occasion to use the latter . . .).

Lack of research into some of the areas we know least about has also been highlighted in this and other publications concerning abuse. The nature and extent of abuse of power in professional relationships and in particular within the Christian community represents one clear gap. More investigation is needed into effective work with offenders, especially young people. In Chapter 1 I identified the need for work around the issue of teenage sexual relationships and the issue of peer abuse. I have struggled to find many well-researched and illuminating accounts of survivors' experiences, beyond very personal testimonies (valuable as these have been). There are still many gaps in our knowledge of effective healing methods, especially concerning mental, emotional and spiritual health. Perhaps the final significant area needing more work is prevention generally; what can we do to avoid creating abusive relationships in the first place?

Creative initiatives

The last area to highlight I would call creative initiatives. I fear that I have also been guilty of institutionalized thinking in some of the areas I have emphasized in this publication. Abuse of power is a complex and fundamental dynamic that demands rich and creative responses. Maybe if we did more to listen to the voices of the people whose lives are directly affected by abuse, we might encourage more imaginative lateral thinking. As well as individual counselling, how about more focused short-life groups, maybe dealing with a specific issue like dissociation, maybe using more holistic techniques such as art, drama, writing and meditation to inspire healing and growth? In treatment of offenders, how can we truly model restorative justice by involving victims and their supporters in treatment and reparation programmes? In community events and programmes, how can we give space to survivors to share their experiences and support each other? In living out our global citizenship, how do we exchange the lessons learnt from different contexts of abuse and establish networks of survivors and community leaders? In safety programmes, how do we involve children and young people in creating and sharing their own strategies? The challenge of our God of surprises is to widen our vision and encourage the unexpected, in this upside-down Kingdom of his.

Yearning and ritual

In specifically Christian contexts, we can create special opportunities to consciously sit with God on these issues. I believe we do God's work all the time in all places, and the spiritual is as much a focus of my work time as when I am in the gathered Christian community. Worship happens when I talk to a survivor on the phone who needs the reassurance of a friendly voice and a listening ear, as much as when I sing a song of love or justice in a church service. But just as the best conversations contain as many pauses as words, sometimes I need to stop and be with God to really experience the Kingdom. Worship, house groups, prayer times, rituals and actions all provide these opportunities.

These are very practical things we can do quite easily: creating Bible studies and sermons that relate to abuse and the issues laid out in this book; holding workshops and discussion groups to raise awareness; creating prayer initiatives such as designating a special space for prayers about abuse or holding a focused prayer time; inviting survivors and those working in the field to participate in special services and rituals to mourn, rage, heal and celebrate together.

One of the important considerations to hold in mind when creating such opportunities is not to feel we have to provide neat answers or solutions to every issue surrounding abuse. These are spaces for expressing our yearning for justice and restoration certainly. I believe the instinct for that yearning towards a life of thriving comes from dwelling in the pain of reality as much as from dreaming of hope. Here is the place of the triune God; the Christ-Accompanist who enters the messiness and suffering; the Parent-Creator who mourns and rages, heals and tenderly holds us; the Spirit of the long haul who brings strength and endurance, hope and transformation.

DISCUSSION QUESTIONS

To discuss
What struck you most about the healing journey described? Have you had experience of some of the stumbling blocks? Can you see yourself or your friends in any of the images of companionship offered?

To reflect
The cycle of relinquishment and reshaping applies to all of us in our growing, not just abuse survivors. What, at this point in your life, is it time for you to leave behind? Into what new shape are you growing? You might like to model this using clay or plasticine.

To do
There are many suggestions in this chapter for both individual and community action to support survivors. Is there one that speaks loudly enough to you that you can start putting it into practice? It may be simply that you can offer more support to someone you know who has experienced abuse. Another good starting point is offering to help a community initiative that already exists, such as a helpline or support group.

Notes

1   Margaret Kennedy, an acknowledged expert in this field, used this phrase at the launch of the *Time for Action* report (see references).
2   A saying from the Congo.
3   A reference to C. S. Lewis's series of books about the imaginary world of Narnia.
4   See, for example, Moltmann, J., *Theology of Hope: on the Grounds and Implications of Christian Eschatology* (new edn), London, SCM Press, 2002.
5   Emma Robinson, 2003, quoted with permission.
6   For example, NCH Report: Bywaters, P. and Rolfe, A., *Look Beyond the Scars: understanding and responding to self-injury and self-harm.* NCH, 2002, available to download from <http://www.nch.org/selfharm>.
7   Emma Robinson, 2003, written submission to the author, quoted with permission.

8 A term developed by Alice Miller, Ph.D. to describe a helping witness who assists a survivor to recognize and deal with abuse and to gain a notion of trust and love. See, for example, <http://www.naturalchild .com/alice_miller/witness.html>.
9 Dr Elia Vecchione, Ph.D., of Upper Valley Services in Vermont, quoted in Pitonyak, 2002.
10 Revd Dave Gardner, sermon series preached January–February 2004. You can download sermon notes from the church website <http:// www.stjohnswoodbridge.org.uk>.

References

Bywaters, P. and Rolfe, A., *Look Beyond the Scars: Understanding and responding to self-injury and self-harm*, National Children's Home (NCH) Report, 2002.
Economic and Social Research Council (ESRC), Children 5–16 Research Briefing, No. 12, April 2000, *Children's Needs, Coping Strategies and Understanding of Woman Abuse*, University of Stirling, 2000.
Ford, D., *Self and Salvation, Being Transformed*, Cambridge University Press, Cambridge, 1999.
Gosney, J., *Surviving Child Sexual Abuse: Supporting Adults in the Church*, Grove Books, Cambridge, 2002.
Green, M. and Christian, C., *Accompanying Young People on their Spiritual Quest*, The National Society/Church House Publishing, London, 1998.
McFadyen, A., *Bound to Sin: Abuse, Holocaust and the Christian Doctrine of Sin*, Cambridge University Press, Cambridge, 2000.
Nydam, R., *Adoptees Come of Age: living within two families*, Westminster John Knox Press, Louisville, KY, 1999.
Obbard, E. R., *Medieval Women Mystics*, New City Press, New York, 2002.
Pitonyak, David, *Supporting a Person Who Is Experiencing Post Traumatic Stress Disorder (PTSD)*, 2002, <http://www.vcu.edu/ rrtcweb/cyberu/ webcast/trausept.pdf>, accessed 4 December 2003.
Strong, M., *A Bright Red Scream: self-mutilation and the language of pain*, Virago, London, 2000.
Time for Action: Sexual abuse, the Churches and a new dawn for survivors, The Report to Churches Together in Britain and Ireland of the Group established to examine issues of Sexual Abuse, Churches Together in Britain and Ireland, London, 2002.

6

Careful Grace:
working with offenders

———◄◦►———

At this, those who heard began to go away one at a time, the older ones first, until only Jesus was left, with the woman still standing there. Jesus straightened up and asked her, 'Woman, where are they? Has no-one condemned you?'

'No-one, sir,' she said.

'Then neither do I condemn you,' Jesus declared. 'Go now and leave your life of sin.'

John 8.9–11

The encounter between Jesus and the woman 'caught' in adultery is a breathtaking vision for a survivor. I initially connect with the woman myself, at the deepest level. I have inherited from the abuse the dynamic of shame and guilt, the self-loathing, the sense of utter contamination that means I certainly do condemn myself and have spiritually, psychologically and physically pelted myself with stones. This is reinforced by the disbelief, denial, silence and inaction of others; or the experience of being treated with suspicion or judgement by people who are uncomfortable with the reality of abuse. Jesus' redemptive acceptance and the promise of a new life speak to my innermost longings, with the compassion and hope that I am unable to offer myself.

The shock of the passage comes with the realization that this compassion and hope are heard with the same profound longing and astonishment by my abuser. The message of redemption is there for both of us, with devastating effect (in the sense that both our lives are turned inside out). That we are both traumatized by the experience of abuse we share, I can just about grasp. That we also share the same path to restoration, in that sense are connected still to each other, is an overwhelmingly disturbing truth. Far easier to hate my abuser, dehumanize or even demonize him, to remain in the safe polarity of opposite extremes; or perhaps I can manage the polite forgiveness of indifferent disinterest. It is disturbing indeed to recognize our shared humanity and the interdependence of our liberation from the captivity of the abuse. Trevor Dennis (1999, p. 50) provides another powerful rendering of this insight in his story of 'the Harrowing of Hell' where he imagines Hitler's saviour, a tiny child of the concentration camps, called Leah: 'You must let her take you out of here,' Christ informs Hitler. 'She knows the way. She is very wise for her years. She will lead you, and when you are out of this terrible dark, I will find you myself and take you home.'

This realization of the abuser's humanity is tempered by a concern for the survivors, children and adults, women and men, who have survived but suffered, who have failed to survive, who are still to become victims, who are being abused right this moment. Churches have been known as safe havens for offenders and certainly the opportunity for redemption that Christianity offers is in striking contrast to the 'name and shame' culture and punitive demands of our society. It is a brave and extraordinary act to promote the Christian message, which speaks of unconditional love, and the new life of grace God gives us, whatever our sin. We recognize that a harsh justice threatens our capacity to give and receive charity: 'we do pray for mercy, and that same prayer doth teach us all to render the deeds of mercy.'[1] But also we need to be careful not to offer grace too cheaply or hastily in our human relationships. The generosity of God's grace does not obviate the need to hold to account, set boundaries and fulfil our responsibilities to protect the vulnerable.

Communities and churches need to tread a careful path to provide justice and grace for both people who abuse and those whom they abuse. The relationship between redemption, forgiveness, confession and reparation may not be a dependent one, but the links are certainly strong. These connections and their implications need to underpin our actions. Our theological understanding may be that forgiveness is not dependant on remorse, for example; but, equally, redemption is clearly accompanied by a call to a new life, as with the woman caught in adultery. So we temper our offer to everyone accused or convicted of a crime (or sin) the welcome of a new start with the understanding that we expect the new life to include new behaviour. Seeking a better understanding of what we are dealing with, and clarifying our underlying principles, assists us in this task.

The nature of abuse

Tracking the institutional response of the Christian community to sexual abuse committed by Church leaders can demonstrate the development of our understanding of the nature of abuse. We have moved from seeing it as a sin that needs confession, to a psychological condition that needs treatment, to a compulsion that needs control (see

National Federation for Catholic Youth Ministry (NFCYM), 2002). Our response has grown from absolution through therapy to suspension and restricted boundaries. Only in this last response have we been successful at protecting potential victims and recognizing the need to balance the interests of all involved.

Grubin (1998) points to the fact that it is predisposition (e.g. low social competence, degree of fixation on victims) combined with opportunity (contact with potential victims) that creates offenders and this combined with the level of violence displayed towards victims distinguishes different categories of offenders. This points to the approach we need to adopt when working with offenders; namely, to understand and 'treat' the underlying disposition and reduce the opportunity. This first section of the chapter aims to increase understanding of the abuser before moving on to propose specific strategies to reduce the risk of re-offending.

Understanding offenders

Is there a typical abuser? Most experts appear to propose that abusers fit into two distinctive categories. There is the habitual, predatory offender, who may be described as having a pathological character defect. This is someone who will have more than one victim, may expend considerable effort and energy into targeting and manipulating victims to suit his desires, and is normally considered as having a permanent predilection, that is, there will always be a need to contain and control his behaviour. Second, there is the situational abuser, who may be a sexual wanderer, may revert to violence under stress, and may be a victim of abuse herself who is acting out her experience or repeating learnt/conditioned behaviour. These abusers are likely only to have one victim and once the underlying issues within their situation have been addressed, we can conclude that they have no more reason than the rest of us to abuse again. Of course just as the journey with survivors is an enduring one, there are no quick fixes for offenders either. Like someone dependent on alcohol, recognizing and admitting to the problem is the first vital step towards changing behaviour, and this point may not be reached for a long time. Some have suggested a third category, the lover. This is the normal leader who is not already in a committed relationship and happens to fall in love with someone under his or her care. The situation becomes abusive if the boundaries of role are ignored and the relationship develops rapidly despite the power inequalities and potential imbalance in the wider group dynamics.

I have not read any research or expert opinion that can completely convince me there is such a clear distinction between these twin faces of abusers. It makes more sense to me to recognize a continuum of behaviour that is affected by a complex variety of factors. At one end is the abusive behaviour I can see in myself on an average 'bad hair day', when I slam doors, frighten the cat, say hurtful things to my family and drive aggressively. At the other is the repeated extreme predilection of people like Fred and Rose West.[2] Although there is clear evidence that the latter group do not easily emerge from our justice system as completely reformed individuals, their humanity remains undisputed. Is it just to condemn them for ever? Re-conviction rates are not demonstrably higher for abuse offenders than the average rate for other types of offence, apart from a small minority of very high-risk sexual and violent offenders, with recidivism rates of 25–50 per cent. Treatment programmes have been shown to be modestly successful, but need to be combined in a multi-agency approach with both harm reduction and attempts to address the primary causes (Grubin, 1998).

The abuser's cycle
Certain patterns of abusive behaviour are evident from a comparison of research on perpetrators of domestic violence and sexual offences.[3] This helps us to understand some of the key dynamics we need to address when dealing with known offenders in our churches, organizations, communities and families. These patterns are warning signals for recognizing an abusive situation as it starts to develop and indicate behaviour to be prepared for when working with habitual offenders. The learning we gain from understanding offending behaviour can help us in both prevention and harm reduction.

The table in Figure 4 gives a picture of an abusive situation that develops, rather than arriving unannounced. There are events in both the external world and the internal life of the abuser that are part of the stage I have called 'preparation'. The motivation to abuse is present – stress may be developing, historical or personality factors may create a predilection. Permission to abuse also comes from cultural expectation (e.g. it is acceptable to discipline children) and is fuelled by previous (successful) experience of abusing. Fantasy and labelling help to overcome the braking power of the conscience; for example, an abuser will rationalize that the victim deserves the abuse or that it doesn't really harm them. In abusive groups and homes, opportunity is nurtured in environments that allow secrecy, dependency and restrictive cultural norms. This opportunity to abuse is deliberately created: families may be discouraged from developing friendships or any activities outside of the home, leaders seek to normalize one-to-one contact, child molesters volunteer for youth work. In the context of child abuse and abuse by leaders in particular, this leads into a process of targeting and 'grooming' intended victims. Establishing secrecy and creating confusion help to overcome the resistance of the victim. She/he may be too young or too vulnerable to really appreciate what is happening until

Domestic violence	Sexual offences
Preparation	
Tension Builds	*Fantasy and Unblocking*
• Perpetrator fails to recognize build in tension	• Perpetrator has motivation to abuse
• S/he withdraws or escapes into work	• Fantasizes about illegal sexual activity
• Uses 'labelling'[1] to reduce victim to object of lesser importance	• Internal (conscience) and external (opportunity) inhibitors are overcome
• May perceive the victim as defying authority	• Fantasy and masturbation develop the urge to offend
Abuse	
Explosion	*Grooming and Sexual Abuse*
• Verbal abuse may escalate into physical violence	• Victim is identified and 'groomed'[2]
• Coercion/intimidation used to establish control	• Level of abuse is usually progressive
• May be trigger, e.g. stress, perceived disobedience	• May be specific trigger to repeated cycles of abuse
Aftermath	
Regret/Respite	*Pause/React to feelings*
• May regret behaviour and show remorse/apologize	• May experience guilt/fear of consequences
• May minimize/blame victim/reject responsibility	• Further fantasy/masturbation reinforces permission to abuse
• Cycle may repeat, escalating control and violence, spread to children and pets	• Abuse may escalate rapidly
	• Often many further victims

1 Attaching labels that put down and blame, e.g. slag, bastard, hysterical, incompetent.
2 Using manipulative and coercive techniques with the victim(s) and those who might protect them, to create opportunity and prevent disclosure or discovery.

Figure 4   The cycle of abuse

it is too late; or may not have the understanding or confidence to say 'No'. The isolation ensures the victim has no one to tell; or perhaps he is especially vulnerable due to age (the youngest and oldest), disability, previous abuse or cultural environment (for example, Asian women and black young people have less reason to seek outside assistance and to trust that authorities will intervene positively). This does not mean the victim is responsible for the abuse, but does make it even easier for the perpetrator.

The abuse itself commonly develops in force and intensity. A slap may precede a beating; a touch paves the way for rape and buggery; a manipulative scriptural message may lead to total spiritual domination. The escalation is often subtle and gradual, which makes it much harder to recognize until the victim is so committed as to feel trapped. He may not reveal his physically violent nature until you are married. She may be the friendliest of baby-sitters and you enjoy the cuddles and the physical play. By the time she puts her hand on your penis, you feel like you've already said yes and she is a trusted member of your family. They may be the most charismatic, attentive and convincing leaders. You will have given your trust, friendship and respect to them as mentors before you realize it is their will, their rules, not God's you have to follow. It is likely this will be reinforced by punishment and subtle manipulation, even mind control techniques. Disciples who question or disobey are punished, often openly humiliated. Publicly, it may be claimed that dis-agreement is tolerated; in fact, it is made clear that if you disagree you are not just misguided but heretical, sinful, even possessed. In an abusive home, you are constantly belittled and both you and the children are threatened with death if you attempt to leave (there is clear evidence that these are not empty threats). As a sexually abused child, you are told that if you try to tell you will be punished, treats will be withdrawn, no one will believe you, you will be responsible for the break-up of the family. This diminution reduces the value of the victim to sub-human. The shame and guilt experienced by the victim reinforces this self-image. Society's tendency to minimize the effects of the abuse colludes with this distortion of the truth.

In the aftermath of an abusive episode, the abuser may feel some immediate guilt, express remorse and promise not to repeat their offence. But this is short-lived, and soon they are blaming the victim and minimizing the effect, or fantasizing again, back in the preparation stage of the cycle. You asked for it, you are stupid, a slag, looked provocative, need your sexuality awakening, aren't prepared to (spiritually) change, aren't committed enough, are listening to yourself and not God. The profound effect all this has on the people being abused was explained in Chapter 2. The abuser is freed from responsibility for what happens and moves back to the beginning of the cycle, repeating the abuse; each time round the level of abuse is likely to escalate. Control and contempt seem to reproduce themselves like cancerous cells; thus abusive behaviour becomes addictive. Other victims may be chosen, from partner to children and pets, from a single chosen favourite to a handpicked group; unwittingly, victims may introduce other potential targets through invitations to visit the abuser's group or family.

The abuser's personality

In Chapter 1, we looked at some of the central ideas about what causes abuse. The three main themes to emerge started with the recognition that a complex range of environmental and historical factors can pre-dispose someone to abuse. Second, we identified a culture that gives subtle permission to abuse and creates the ideal conditions for abuse to grow. Suggestions to establish a non-abusive culture follow in Chapters 7 and 8. Finally we considered personal factors that might prompt or sustain a tendency towards abusive behaviour. This section focuses on these personality traits.

The fact that not all abusers have themselves been abused means we are not just dealing with learnt behaviour. It also adds credence to the proposition that some internal qualities make the difference between someone who abuses and those who, in similar circumstances, succeed in breaking out of a pattern of abuse. Research does not substantiate the popular image of offenders as socially deficient, unattractive personalities. In fact, many successful abusers have charismatic personae, which is why they are able to attract their victims and charm the rest of the surrounding community into disbelief or abuse-blindness. This is particularly true of abusers in positions of authority in churches and other institutions. It is the popular leader, not the social pariah, who is the typical abuser; normally the last person we expect.

Many sex offenders report isolation and a lack of intimacy in regular relationships. However, this does not mean that they are unsuccessful in achieving sexual relations with others, so the offending behaviour is not merely filling a straightforward gap in their lives; it is just an easier way to overcome emotional loneliness (Gibbs, 1992; Grubin, 1998). The isolation of the perpetrator may be a factor in the stress that commonly builds up to a trigger point when the abuse occurs. There is evidence that sexual deviancy is present in the more persistent and aggressive offenders. Self-perception is often highly unrealistic, even though they may be very self-preoccupied. Certainly a core characteristic of any abuser is the extreme and deliberate self-interest at the cost of any recognition of the other's needs and desires. The abuser may also have a low self-image combined with poor social perception skills, which result in a distorted interpretation of what they observe (e.g. reading friendliness as sexual advances – see Gibbs, 1992). This means they will consistently succeed in convincing themselves that they have done nothing wrong, even when faced with strong evidence to the contrary. Current treatment programmes frequently include a section on victim empathy, although recently there has been some question as to whether this is the significant factor in reform that it was once thought to be.

Female perpetrators of all types of abuse are still a small minority, even when we look at self-reporting by abusers and survivors, not just convicted offenders. What is clearly demonstrated, for example in the recent Ian Huntley case, is that some may themselves be victims caught up in the controlling, false environment the abuser has constructed. This is increasingly recognized within domestic violence situations, where mothers were in the past seen as partially or equally culpable with their partner, accused of failing to protect their children. Although parents cannot ever morally abdicate their responsibility to care for their offspring, we now understand better that a non-abusing partner (or one eventually drawn into the abuse) may also be under the control of the abuser, or genuinely unable to perceive and absorb the reality of the situation they are in. However, we need to separate this understanding from respecting the experience of the victim(s). To the child abused by their mother, the effect is the same whether she or the father was the initiator of the abuse. Also, in recognizing the higher risk that men pose, we should avoid minimizing or denying the reality of abuse by women and its equally devastating consequences. As previously highlighted, a man abused by his wife, or a boy abused by his mother are affected just as powerfully by the abuse itself and face the compounding baggage of confronting the stereotypical male 'macho' image.

It is not possible to give one set of generalized characteristics that are shared by all abusers. Some patterns do emerge from research with offenders, victims and agencies working with abusers at all stages of discovery, investigation, punishment and treatment. Those I have not already mentioned are worth highlighting:

• Personal (including sexual) problems and difficulties with intimacy can be a causal factor.
• High levels of hostility and aggression in violent offenders can be predictive indicators, worse if linked with access to weapons (Kemshall, 2001).
• Offending behaviour is commonly repeated; it provides the short-term gratification the offender seeks.
• Chaotic and unstable lifestyles are linked clearly with re-offending rates (Middleton, 2003).
• In leadership, unclear boundaries between the personal and professional life.
• A fundamentalist mindset that focuses on absolutes and discourages self-awareness.
• An inability to empathize with the victim(s).

Environmental factors in an organization that can contribute to abusive behaviour will be discussed further in Chapters 7 and 8.

Strategies for working with known offenders

These guidelines are intended primarily for churches and organizations that have a known offender within their membership. The main strategies may also be useful for families and friendship groups facing the same range of issues. As with supporting survivors, this is an area where specialist knowledge is vital, and in addition to the advice given here, guidance should also be sought from appropriate national and local agencies, such as denominational headquarters, probation services and specialist organizations such as the NSPCC or Women's Aid.

The Probation Service is a key national agency, with responsibility for both the rehabilitation of offenders and public protection. Today, the approach to convicted abusers combines both treatment and risk management. There is an acknowledgement that a total 'cure' is often not a realistic goal; hence there is a 'harm reduction' approach, similar to that adopted in work on drug and alcohol abuse. This is a model of community protection that balances the needs of the individual with those of the wider society. Specific treatment programmes run both during and after custodial sentences, to reduce re-offending.

These programmes are combined with a multi-agency approach to risk management and offender support, thus addressing both internal factors (self-knowledge and self-control) and external issues including opportunity, monitoring and supervision. This approach, formalized through protocols such as the Multi Agency Public Protection Arrangements (MAPPA), helps to ensure that key information is shared and that enforcement and support agencies work together to ensure the best outcomes for both the offender and the community. These are expert agencies working with specialist knowledge and clear responsibilities. However churches and community groups also have a role to play in both risk management and treatment; and can use the knowledge of the experts to inform their own approach. Some denominations and agencies have already published detailed guidelines, and where appropriate these should also be consulted (see Resources in Chapter 10). The following suggestions provide general guidance for a range of situations, and will need to be adapted to meet the specific needs of the context and the nature of the abuse.

Risk assessment

There are four ways we might become aware of an abuser within a church or community group:

- the abuser was already a member when the abuse was disclosed
- another agency notifies us as part of their risk management process
- the abuser discloses to us themselves
- we discover the abuse through background checks undertaken as part of risk prevention strategy

As with the disclosure of the abuse, it is important not to create a hierarchy of information sources. An abuser previously known to us (perhaps even a former leader of the church, for example) is not necessarily less dangerous than a convicted offender who has just moved into our area. Nor does the absence of a criminal record mean that the risk posed is significantly lower, as demonstrated in Chapter 1. Each case should be considered with equal gravity and fairness, on the particular information available.

The first step is to evaluate the information available in order to identify:

- the nature and level of risk indicated by past offending behaviour
- the level of risk particular to the situation and activities of the organization (by level of risk I mean the likelihood of it happening and the potential harm likely to result)

This will almost certainly mean gathering further information and seeking guidance from specialist agencies and those already involved in supervising the offender, where there has been an official investigation. In the case of abuse that does not currently feature within our civil or criminal legal system (such as spiritual abuse), it is vital to take advice from appropriate experts and those involved in any internal investigation. There are now a number of risk assessment specialists (within both statutory services and independent agencies), and unless you have someone with this expertise it is worth investigating how they can be accessed in your locality (for example, social services regarding child abuse, the probation service regarding sex offences generally). These agencies have a variety of specialist tools available to assist risk assessment. There are two main types: a statistical approach (i.e. general risk predictions based on research information) or a clinical assessment (i.e. a diagnostic assessment of the individual in their environment). A recent review of methods used with sexual and violent offenders confirmed that a combination of approaches is most effective and preferred (Kemshall, 2001).

The risk assessment will need to identify areas of high, medium and low risk and work out a strategy to manage these. Each will need to be treated in an appropriate way. A general approach to adopt would be:

- strict measures to avoid high-risk scenarios altogether
- clear measures to reduce medium level risks, open to review thus allowing for progress in self-management
- support to enable the abuser to take increasing responsibility for managing their own behaviour and retaining full membership of the community

For example, the risks associated with a convicted sexual offender will focus on the potential for contact with children and young people and vulnerable adults. The strategy may start with very clear management measures addressing areas of high risk: the abuser will never hold any positions of responsibility that allow them unsupervised contact with this group, for example, a children's worker. Particularly if the nature of the offending behaviour indicates that the risk of re-offending is high, medium risk areas may also be included in a restrictive contract: the offender will agree not to attend all-age services, where informal contact with children may be normalized, until there is some evidence to justify such a degree of trust. This is supported by preventative measures: regular meetings with a group of supporters who help the offender to sustain any treatment programme he is undertaking, deal with any wider personal issues (such as housing, employment, etc.) and provide pastoral and spiritual support to sustain a new life free from abuse.

Risk management

Once assessed, a clear contract is the foundation of the management of risk. This should be negotiated between the abuser and somebody in a leadership position with the appropriate skills and training to monitor its implementation. It will include both conditions and support, on a rights and responsibilities model. The following areas could be included:

- a clear understanding of any role boundaries, for example around membership, positions of responsibility, the role of any supporters
- a confidentiality agreement
- any restrictions on behaviour and involvement
- what is unacceptable behaviour
- what might demonstrate progress and re-earn trust
- what support the abuser will be provided with
- expected involvement with a treatment programme
- monitoring and evaluation processes
- involvement of other agencies
- expectations of the organization
- what the offender is entitled to

These last two categories may include expectations of full participation in any treatment programmes and a commitment to moving towards repentance and reparation. The entitlement might encompass a commitment to respect and equality as a neighbour, on the 'to each according to his/her needs' model of equitable treatment.

Achieving the correct balance between restricted confidentiality and information sharing is an extremely tricky task, complicated by Human Rights and Data Protection legislation. The general rule is that personal data is not shared without permission from the person concerned, unless it is necessary to do so to protect others, particularly the most vulnerable. The foundations of a good risk assessment process will help to identify and justify any information sharing thought necessary to achieve satisfactory harm prevention. The standard principle of only disclosing information on a 'need to know' basis is still a good strategy here. This can go against some church cultures, where public confessions are used as a model of accountability (or sometimes a means of control). A useful distinction to make is between public and private behaviour. Areas of public concern (e.g. a sex offender posing a risk to children) have accountability in the public arena (so will need to be shared with a children's worker or youth leader, for example). Personal issues that don't necessarily impact on others (e.g. alcohol abuse) don't need to be shared outside of the support and accountability structure created. They may still, as in this example, be closely linked with the likelihood of re-offending and so are of concern to those responsible for monitoring and support. Obviously, it will depend on the abuser and the context which category different issues fall into.

Treatment

Most of the arenas of abuse covered in this book require specialist treatment, which the average church, community group or family are not equipped to provide without expert training and support. It is therefore important that we recognize that:

- any pastoral care or prayer ministry we offer should be in addition to, not instead of, participation in an appropriate treatment programme
- such participation should be an expectation we stress in the contract we have with the offender

There are, in the church particularly, some notable examples of when these principles have not been followed. I do not see this as any different to the approach to recognized medical conditions: we might pray for someone to experience God's healing from cancer, but we wouldn't normally expect them to stop any hospital treatment. Healing ministries that don't accept expert intervention are to my mind controlling, dangerous and arrogant in the assumption that God only works through their efforts. Many Christians working in the caring professions undoubtedly feel the same!

Generally, then, our role is likely to be one of support and accountability, complementing specialist intervention; this is discussed further in the next section. The major exception to this occurs when we are dealing with abuse that does not come within a legal framework, such as abuse of trust that falls outside the new legislation (for example, sexual misconduct with adults), or spiritual abuse. I have not been able to discover any established intervention programmes in the UK to deal with such issues, so these are untested ideas I am offering. My suggestions are based on the lessons learnt from the specialist programmes that already exist.

Preconditions to intervention

The efficacy of treatment for abusers has been contentious; however, latest research does indicate that cognitive behavioural approaches particularly are effective in reducing re-offending rates. Identification of the key factors in success rates (Kemshall, 2001; Grubin, 1998) gives us a set of preconditions to put in place before embarking on any programme of intervention.

1 *An appropriate, tested and consistent treatment programme:* it must be a matter of some urgency for the major denominations and Christian organizations with appropriate skills, such as counselling services, to create and pilot a suitable programme for abusers within the Christian community.
2 *Accurate identification of high-risk offenders:* targeting resources where most needed means gaining an accurate picture of the problem. This will depend on having an effective disciplinary procedure and an accessible complaints process so the picture does not remain hidden. The risk assessment process can then be used to identify those individuals who need the extra intervention of an intensive programme. The warning signs of potential abuse, such as overwork, poor boundaries, etc. can be dealt with through normal supervision and support structures (providing these are in place – see Chapter 7).
3 *Early treatment but not whilst in denial:* like any 'talk therapy' or training, someone who attends with a closed mind is unlikely to learn anything of value. There may be some preparation work needed with the individual that addresses the reality of the situation from a 360-degree perspective, challenging any denial of the evidence. Denial of responsibility is an issue that will be confronted during the programme.
4 *An offender with the incentive to change:* in work with violent and sex offenders this refers to a psychological motivation to change. Within a Christian context, we might be looking for a desire to make necessary atonement and move towards restoring a right relationship with God. I think there is also an issue of affirming hope; the abuser needs a vision of what might be the positive outcomes from the treatment programme, the 'living beyond' we have desired for the victim-survivor. This may need to include very practical incentives for employed staff in particular, such as future housing and employment possibilities if treatment is 'successful'. Of course this must recognize the danger of providing a 'tick box' easy option that doesn't facilitate real transformation. Also defining 'successful' and the indicators to measure it will be a challenging task.
5 *Tight monitoring during the programme:* with convicted offenders this may include supervision orders, electronic tagging etc. as well as regular meetings with a supervising officer to monitor progress. In a Christian community there could be an accountability structure set up that reports to the community leadership, generally tasked to the

same group who undertook the risk assessment. Given our understanding of the manipulative nature of some abusers and the
tendency we have to collude with 'quick fix' outcomes, the assistance of an independent agent would also be helpful. An outside
consultant could work with the monitoring group to ensure the
reliability and integrity of the process. Equally, the abuser will
benefit from the support of an independent person, such as a
spiritual director or counsellor, who can accompany them on their
personal journey of recovery.

Treatment aims

An overview of intervention programmes for convicted abusers provides
the strategic objectives and core curriculum for a treatment programme
(Home Office, 2002). The four main aims should include:

1 *Increasing the motivation to stop abusing:* I have already pointed to
   the role of external incentives. Here the focus is on the internal
   impulse to transform and reform. Again there are echoes of the
   survivor's journey, the movement from relinquishment to reshaping.
2 *Gaining insight into one's thoughts, feelings and behaviour:* in youth
   work and other 'people' vocations, the skill of becoming a 'reflective
   practitioner' is a core competence in professional training. It encompasses the ability to reflect on your own values and attitudes,
   identify how these are impacting on your practice and deal with any
   areas that are adversely affecting your work. Tools such as journals
   and practice supervision are key to developing good reflective,
   analytical and evaluative skills.
3 *Increasing the ability to control thoughts and behaviour:* the other
   key process of reflective practice is to engage in a continual process
   of evaluating your work and applying the learning gained. This
   should provide an underpinning for developing a range of strategies
   that move towards sustained non-abusive behaviour.
4 *Developing skills and strategies to manage self and reduce risk:* these
   strategies need to be SMART: *s*pecific, *m*easurable, *a*chievable,
   *r*ealistic, *t*imed. The goal is for the offender to take responsibility for
   managing his or her own life without abuse.

Treatment curriculum

Developing a core curriculum into workable practice is beyond the
scope of this publication and should not be attempted without expert
assistance. The Lucy Faithfull Foundation is the main independent
agency offering assistance for work with sexual offenders. The Prevention of Professional Abuse Network (POPAN) offers training aimed to
prevent abuse of trust in professional relationships and could provide
useful consultancy. I have not been able to discover any programmes set

up to offer counsel or training for Christian leaders who have spiritually abused, although the Claybury Trust does offer a professional
counselling service and personal development course to those in
ministry. Some mainstream Church headquarters may be able to give
assistance; or key organizations working with cults and their victims
could contribute relevant experience. Perhaps it is time a Christian
agency was established to assist with this area of work?

What follows are recommended core curriculum areas that will need
to be tailored to the specific context of the church or organization. These
can provide a syllabus for an intervention programme that may be used
with an individual, or perhaps a group of abusers within a regional or
national scheme. Good practice with convicted offenders, as identified by
the Home Office and other key agencies, has informed these suggestions.

1 *Challenging distorted thinking that is used to justify or excuse
   offending:* this needs to include developing an understanding of the
   dynamics of abuse and recognizing the reality of the abusive
   behaviour as viewed by the community. It will focus on the processes of denial, acknowledgement and responsibility. Cognitive-
   behavioural approaches are proven to be effective in this area.

2 *Victim empathy and understanding how offending behaviour affects
   other people:* as I understand it, this is the reciprocal process of recognizing the other's humanity that I described from the perspective
   of the survivor at the beginning of the chapter. For some abusers it
   may be the first recognition of their own survivor status and the
   development of compassion for themselves. I would like to propose
   that a radical programme that takes seriously the Christian calling
   to reconciliation and shalom, could involve victims in this area of
   treatment. This would need careful management and protection for
   all parties concerned. There should not be pressure on victims to
   participate, and I suggest it should not normally involve anyone with
   a personal connection with the offender – enabling 'anonymous'
   relationships. The notion of 'victim impact' assessments is already in
   the arena of restorative justice and needs to consider the family and
   secondary victims in the wider community as well as survivors.

3 *Recognizing risk factors and triggers:* this covers personal factors
   particular to the individual's situation; and generic factors that can
   be associated with the role and environment. In ministry, these
   include stresses on marriage and personal relationships; the rescuing
   tendency endemic in caring professions; workaholism and
   boundary issues; the demands of an unrealistic/dependent congregation or organization that feed these issues. Theological and cultural
   paradigms that are used to justify the abuse also need to be
   addressed.

4 *Creating strategies for successful lives without offending:* this should

address both personal behaviours and strategies, and the external support and further training and practice needed to achieve a position of persistent non-abusive behaviour. This may mean a changed heart – true transformation or, initially, a sustained avoidance of temptation.

Treatment framework

The 'Time for Action' Report Group suggest a healing journey for offenders that echoes the journey for survivors explored in Chapter 3. This suggests a framework within which the intervention programme can take place, encompassing the wider issues of accountability and support discussed elsewhere in this chapter.

The Group describe the processes in the key (bold) words below; the rest are my additions and I have changed their order to suggest a cycle of healing.

1 **Denial:** both before and during treatment, the offender needs to be encouraged to confront the reality of the abuse as understood by everyone affected and to accept their part in the situation. Equally, the wider community needs to recognize the part it may have played in triggering or colluding with the abuse (such as unrealistic demands on those in ministry).

2 **Treatment:** whether group work or individual counselling or spiritual direction, the abuser needs the same committed accompanying as the victim, as well as the abundance of God's grace. Organizations also need to address the stresses and weaknesses that may have contributed to the abuse.

3 **Justice:** restorative justice can be recognized as central to the healing of the abuser, providing a release from the burden of guilt. This process may parallel treatment or may follow it, once the offender has moved from denial to acceptance of responsibility and a willingness to face the consequences of the abuse. Again, the same is true for the organization or church where the abuse took place.

4 **Atonement:** just as a survivor cannot be rushed into forgiveness, neither should an abuser be a pressurized penitent. I imagine that this is very much a goal of healing that echoes the letting go of forgiveness and may be reached towards the end of the journey. This could take place in the setting of worship or public ritual, which would enable the wider community to participate in this reorientation towards God's Kingdom.

5 **Reparation:** shouldering responsibility and seeking the restoration of shalom implies making active attempts to repair the damage. I talked before about restoring joy in broken lives. These lives include the victim, the families of both the victim and the abuser, and the wider community affected by the abuse. The ultimate restoration,

always offered, is with God; the healing that is not ours to give, only to orientate ourselves towards and give thanks for.

6   **Reconstruction of trust:** as the abuse of power is the ultimate abuse of trust, so the conscious attempt to restore trust is an essential step on the healing journey. The experience of organizations from the arenas of mediation and reconciliation has something useful to offer here. At its most basic, I understand the process of reconciliation to arise from the repeated open and attentive listening of all parties to each other's stories. This leads to the fullest understanding of the position each other inhabits and the possibility of achieving respect, tolerance and change.

Accountability and mentoring

The abuser is most likely to be successful in sustaining reformed behaviour if she/he is given good support as well as being held accountable during the rehabilitation process. Most agencies suggest that a suitably trained and skilled support group is appointed within the church or organization, to provide pastoral support, prayer and practical assistance. A model for this is provided by a recent community-based initiative, 'Circles of Support and Accountability', currently being piloted in three areas of England. These seek to provide a community-based support network for the offender, combating social isolation and providing a supportive environment for growth and rehabilitation. Based on a model pioneered in Canada by the Mennonite Church, and now widely established there, it could reduce re-offending rates by as much as 50 per cent.

The concept is simple and essentially biblical. The Circle, comprised of trained volunteers, forms a micro-community around the offender, who becomes the 'core member'. The volunteers offer the total acceptance that affirms the core member's worth as a person and assist reintegration into the community. In addition, the core member is held accountable for their progress and offered practical support to develop social skills and deal with issues such as housing and employment. At the beginning the Circle meets weekly and there is normally daily telephone contact. This will reduce gradually according to the needs of the core member and the accompanying goal of protecting the public. The latter role will at times mean the Circle volunteers challenge behaviour that could indicate a slide towards re-offending and seek ways to resolve the issues raised. This is tough love as well as (in the Mennonite phrase) 'radical hospitality'.[4]

The name is reserved for the pilot groups operating to careful guidelines and professional oversight. However, the model is an essentially gospel-orientated response to the Christian calling to love and reconciliation. The vision of Christian communities across the country offering similar refuge, challenge and life-giving care is an inspirational one. It would also provide a beacon of good practice in the wider arena of all work towards the rehabilitation of offenders, surely one of the largest group of outcasts in today's society.

Thus, a careful path towards reconciliation is crafted, avoiding the 'cheap grace' that Bonhoeffer warned against. The abusers, who by their actions have separated themselves from God and community, are offered a wide-armed welcome and the option of change. Not, in the end, on the strength of our efforts, of course; as we are reminded, 'We must commend other people wholly and unreservedly to God and leave them in his hands, and transform our anxiety for them into prayers on their behalf: with sorrow and with grief . . . God will not be distracted' (Bonhoeffer, 1971, p. 177).

DISCUSSION QUESTIONS

To discuss
How do you feel about people who abuse others? What do you think should be society's response? What is the place of justice, reparation, mercy and grace?

To reflect
How do you hold yourself accountable to others (and to God)? When have you experienced grace? What do you envisage as the path to redemption for abusers? Do you see any connection with the survivor's journey?

To do
If you are involved in a church or agency that has abusers in membership, perhaps you can contribute to policy development or work to support them. Could you join or even initiate a Circle of Support in your area?

Notes

1   Portia to Shylock; William Shakespeare, *The Merchant of Venice*, Act 4, Scene 1.
2   Fred West killed at least 12 victims between 1967 and the 1990s. He committed suicide before he could be brought to trial. His wife was jailed for ten murders and is serving a life sentence.
3   Particularly significant sources for the table (Fig. 4) include Gibbs (1992), Nixson (1994) and Sullivan (2002). The framework is a basis for understanding individuals' offending behaviour and is not all-inclusive.
4   Sources include Public Protection News (Home Office) 2002 and Foot, D., 'Going Straight in Circles', *Caring* (CCPAS magazine), Winter 2001/2.

References

Bonhoeffer, D., *Letters and Papers from Prison* (enlarged edn), SCM Press, London, 1971.

Dennis, T., *The Three Faces of Christ*, Triangle, London, 1999.

Foot, D., 'Going Straight in Circles', *Caring*, Winter 2001/2.

Gibbs, P., *Child Sexual Abuse, A Concern for the Church?*, Grove Books, Nottingham, 1992.

Grubin, D., *Sex Offending Against Children: Understanding the Risk*, Police and Reducing Crime Unit, London, 1998.

Home Office Report, *The Treatment and Risk Management of Sexual Offenders in Custody and in the Community*, National Probation Directorate, London, 2002.

Kemshall, H., *Risk Assessment and Management of Known Sexual and Violent Offenders: A review of current issues*, Home Office, London, 2001.

Middleton, D., 'Sex Offender Treatment', *Public Protection News*, Issue 5, November 2003.

National Federation for Catholic Youth Ministry (NFCYM) 2002, found on <http://www.nfcym.org/2001/restoring_trust/speaking.html>, accessed 7 October 2003.

Nixson, R., *Home is Where the Hurt is: Domestic violence and the Church's response*, Grove Books, Cambridge, 1994.

Sullivan, J., 'The Spiral of Sexual Abuse', *Snowdrop & MACSAS News*, (combined issue) Summer 2002.

Time for Action: Sexual abuse, the Churches and a new dawn for survivors, The Report to Churches Together in Britain and Ireland of the Group established to examine issues of Sexual Abuse, Churches Together in Britain and Ireland, London, 2002.

7

Vulnerable Leaders: models for good practice in preventing abuse

———◆○▶———

At that time the disciples came to Jesus and asked, 'Who is the greatest in the kingdom of heaven?'
    He called a little child [whom he placed] among them. And he said: 'I tell you the truth, unless you change and become like little children, you will never enter the kingdom of heaven.'

Matthew 18.1–3

The high levels of sexual abuse in the Church can be explained by this combination: powerful but susceptible people with sexual and personal problems, in stressful jobs without boundaries, working with other people often vulnerable and needy and without boundaries, in an organization without training or supervision, in an ecclesiastical culture dominated by sexual shame and endemic secrecy. (*Time for Action*, 2002)

This sharp and succinct picture in relation to sexual offending provides a summary of the organizational weaknesses we need to address to become safer communities, growing safer leaders. It also points to some of the most important strategies we can adopt to prevent such an explosive situation developing. In Chapter 1, the warning signs of an abusive organization were highlighted, and in Chapter 3 the principles on which to build a non-abusive culture were suggested. Here I look at implementation of some model organizational and personal routines that can support good practice. I focus on the conduct of those in leadership and recommend adopting good management practice, based on the model of vulnerable, accountable and transparent leadership as a biblical, ethical, non-abusive and empowering model.

The dynamics of power

Any power relationship is open to abuse, whether that power is gained through force of personality, relationship (such as parent) or the authority of leadership. The advantage of leadership is that your power is strengthened in a number of ways that are not just dependent on your own efforts. There is the status of the role; our postmodern culture has not rejected the concept of leadership altogether, although the younger generations might choose to follow a media star rather than a politician. There is the power of holding perceived authority within a particular office: it seems to me that our attitudes towards politicians still replay our feudal past; the fact that we are surprised or annoyed when we discover their ignorance, ineptitude or lack of moral fibre suggests that we assume they will normally display knowledge, competence and integrity. There is the influential power of participation and ownership in decision-making processes and often the control of resources; this enables the exclusion of dissension and the execution of plans that suit us or make us look or feel good.

Within churches and Christian organizations, there is the added layer of spiritual and moral authority we expect from those in ministry and other forms of leadership. It is woven into the very fabric of Christian leadership, which after all is not merely an appointment or profession nor even an elected position, but a vocation whose validity, whilst also tested and confirmed by the Church, ultimately comes from God. This creates an authority that it is very difficult to question and easy to use to abuse others. The starting point for non-abusive leadership is the recognition of the imbalance of power in all positions of authority, but especially those of religious leaders and anyone engaged in public ministry. In this latter category we can include youth and children's workers, lay ministers, those involved in pastoral care and counselling, healing and prayer ministries, house-group and fellowship leaders, lay readers, evangelists and worship leaders. This means that personal relationships between people in such roles and those they serve cannot be based on mutual consent, because of the imbalance of power. It also means that they are particularly vulnerable to abuse of trust.

The betrayal

The foundation of the relationship between leaders and their followers is trust. It has reciprocal qualities; followers who consistently deviate and pursue their own path will, in sufficient numbers, marginalize and disempower the leader who has counted on their loyalty. But the inequality of the relationship means that the greater trust is from the follower, who is in a more vulnerable position; that their best interests will be served by proceeding where they are led. This implies a pastoral quality some might challenge; indeed there is a vigorous critique of any idea that this picture represents archetypal leadership. A dependent fol-lowership is unhealthy, the argument goes, and removes responsibility from the followers to make decisions about their own lives and face the consequences of their actions. I would support this analysis unequivocally; but I do believe the reality of leadership in our contemporary institutions has yet to change radically. Thus the betrayal of trust is the ultimate exploitation of abusive leadership; just as the restoration of trust is significant in the reconciliation process described in the previous chapter. Paradoxically, it is to the risk of increased vulnerability, rather than rigid safety, that we turn to find a solution to this danger. It is to a life of leadership 'built on a life of prayer, vulnerability and trust, rather than relevance, popularity and power' (Herrick and Mann, 1998).

Vulnerability

At the start of this book I highlighted the particular vulnerability of those who are abused and also the susceptibility of authority figures to take advantage of this. It is perhaps easiest to recognize this among the 'wanderer' and 'lover' archetypes of abuser, within our leadership and ministry workforce. Here is someone responding to a calling that is orientated towards serving others, in a context that places great expectations on their shoulders, often without providing any significant support to lessen the load. These dangers are apparent in many 'people professions', including care work, education and medicine. The question we still need to answer satisfactorily is, who cares for the carer? The community must share responsibility for protecting vulnerable leaders as well as vulnerable 'clients'. The goals of reducing stress, encouraging a balance of work, rest and play, protecting leaders' family and personal life and avoiding unrealistic and impossible demands are ours to strive for, not the leaders' alone. A culture that exploits and dehumanizes its leadership should not be surprised when these traits are replicated by the leaders themselves, pushing the problem further down the chain.

Jesus' answer to this was a surprising one, which seems to contradict the obvious implications of my argument. Far from fighting exploitation with the weapons of strict rules and professional separation, he turned the other cheek and embraced the ultimate exploitation of the cross. This is the incarnational model of powerlessness that Bonhoeffer (1971, p. 360) described:

> God lets himself be pushed out of the world on to the cross. He is weak
> and powerless in the world, and that is precisely the way, the only
> way, in which he is with us and helps us. Matt 8.17 makes it quite clear
> that Christ helps us, not by virtue of his omnipotence, but by virtue of
> his weakness and suffering . . . It is not the religious act that makes the
> Christian, but participation in the sufferings of God in secular life.

How then to achieve this vulnerable leadership, without succumbing to our weakness to abuse or be abused? Just as Jesus relied on God for his strength and guidance, so there are essential things we can do that will help us.

Clarity of role

Good management practice recognizes the importance of clear and realistic job descriptions, which are regularly reviewed within a process of constructive supervision and appraisal. This is often not the case for those in ministry, or for the many volunteers who provide the majority of the person-power in the voluntary sector, particularly within the Christian community. And yet clarity of purpose and responsibility were significant features of Jesus' ministry. He announced his purpose at the beginning and gave a clear commission to his disciples, particularly when he was preparing them to take on responsibilities without his bodily presence. Peter's job description may not be the longest in history, but it is certainly focused. He allowed the disciples to interrogate him about their task and gave them critical feedback on their performance. He used the simple but profound communication of story to help them understand their role and the wider context of the 'organization'. When he could no longer be there to supervise hands-on, he promised – and delivered – the support of the Holy Spirit. These are clear measures we can introduce for both paid and voluntary leadership roles.

Training
Initial training and in-service training needs to be far more focused on equipping people for the role they will undertake, in their vocational context. The implications of preparing people for a non-abusive practice and culture suggest the following areas are essential:

- good management practices, of self, others and the work
- the practice of vulnerable leadership
- ethical principles and practice
- the process of safe practice within the role (e.g. counselling, youth work etc.)
- anti-oppressive practice and empowerment
- recognizing, responding to and preventing abuse

Job descriptions
All official posts within churches and organizations should have a clear description that defines the tasks and boundaries of the role, whether an occasional voluntary task or a full-time paid position. It should be written within the context of an overall plan for the agency, preferably three- or five-year, but even one would do. The job description then

describes the particular function of the individual in achieving that plan, as part of the wider body. It should include:

- the key objectives of the post, summarizing what it is hoped the worker will achieve
- the main tasks the person is expected to undertake, which should be realistically achievable in the time available and able to assist evaluation of progress
- the main responsibilities of the post, such as for personnel or resources, a particular area of work within the organization, any multi-agency arrangements
- expectations of suitable professional behaviour; for example, following a particular code of ethics, participating in the worshipping life of the church (unsuitable behaviour is normally defined in disciplinary procedures, in an employee handbook, or an ethical code)
- the lines of accountability: who the post-holder reports to, relationship with any management bodies, any requirements for regular reporting
- supervision and support arrangements, including spiritual direction, external supervision and so on
- training entitlements and expectations
- appraisal and post-review arrangements

Ethical code

Regulatory bodies for professions like medicine and counselling already have ethical codes that define the expectations of ethical conduct and provide guiding principles for best practice. Often these will include clear consequences for someone found to be in breach of the code, which is independent of any legal or disciplinary procedure that might take place. Churches and youth organizations are also beginning to develop these codes, which may be voluntary guidelines, but are also useful in helping to clarify for everyone what is appropriate conduct and how to deal with some of the ethical issues pertinent to the role. Guidelines for clergy have recently been published by the Church of England, for example and having read them, I commend the work that has gone into their breadth and in particular the exploration of a theological framework. Reading with the eyes of a survivor who tried to report clergy misconduct, there are some criticisms. I suggest that anyone drawing up such guidelines, or incorporating them into safe practice, consults as widely as possible to reflect the perspective of both the 'client' and the 'professional' in defining what is appropriate.

Supervision
It is not enough just to give people training, a job description and an ethical code – and then abandon them to get on with it. Having clarified expectations, there needs to be supervision to ensure:

1 They can do the job – they have the right training, skills, attitude and personality for the role and can develop best practice.
2 The job is do-able – the demands of the agency are realistic, adjusted to changing circumstances, on-vision as well as on-task, appropriately resourced.
3 They are held to account – both for the task and their conduct in striving to achieve it.
4 They are supported – to deal with the demands of the job and the demands of life, particularly as these impact on each other. I believe it is impossible to manage and support someone effectively by committee. Even in a small agency, mostly staffed by volunteers (who in a church, of course, are also members), it should be possible to identify one person who can undertake a 'line manager' role, perhaps supported by small team meetings and an external supervision arrangement.

A clear job description defines the measurements to be used to check that someone is fulfilling their task and functioning competently and appropriately. Line management and supervision provide the context and process for doing the measuring. Supervision is 'a process by which one worker enables another to practise to the best of his/her ability. Supervision takes place when those involved meet in the time set aside to work together on the agreed agenda' (Community Education Service, 1993, p. 9). There are several different models of supervision and the main characteristics of these are outlined below. There are plenty of good resource books written for the church and voluntary sectors that can provide further detailed advice and assistance (see Chapter 10).

Management supervision
Often called line management, this is the supervision of a staff member by someone to whom they are accountable, who may also have authority over them (in terms of promotion, dismissal, etc.) as well as their area of work (for example a youth leader managed by the chair of the youth committee). Management supervision addresses the agenda of the agency as well as the worker. Its main purposes usually include (Sandy Adirondack, 1998):

• monitoring work and work performance
• evaluating work and performance
• helping the worker improve his or her practice

- clarifying priorities
- sharing information about work
- exploring how the worker and supervisor feel about the work
- recognizing and dealing with existing or potential problems
- identifying how outside factors are affecting work
- providing a framework for discussing and agreeing change

Consultant supervision
This is where the supervisor comes from outside of the agency of the supervisee(s). Characteristics of the model are that it is a voluntary relationship, a self-managed process and involves co-operative learning, which helps the worker to learn about themselves and their work (Jenny Broadbent, 1987). This model is also known as non-managerial super-vision and usually involves an experienced professional assisting an individual or a team to reflect on their practice with the objectivity and outside view of someone not from the agency and with no agenda of their own, within a confidential relationship. Independent supervision is a requirement of counsellors in membership of the British Association for Counselling and Psychotherapy and I believe it is essential for anyone in ministry who shares similar vulnerabilities in their role and 'client' group. The advantages of consultant supervision include:

1 Its independence from any organizational agenda, thereby creating a safer space to honestly explore strengths and weaknesses, personal issues that may be affecting safe working practice and possible exploitation by the worker or the agency.
2 Its ability to focus on the needs and agenda of the worker, which may at times be in conflict with the organization's needs and demands.
3 The benefits of stepping back from immediate work performance issues, and reflecting on the whole person, with an emphasis on growth and learning rather than achievement.
4 There is still an accountability from supervisee to supervisor, but it is a voluntary relationship and the ownership rests with the super-visee, thus encouraging personal responsibility.

Peer supervision
I use this term to describe two or more colleagues of equivalent status from the same agency, normally from the same team, who agree to meet to reflect on their practice in a reciprocal arrangement. It could also be a relationship with a peer in a neighbouring project or church, for example, although the dual relationships of co-supervision can lead to collusion ('I'll overlook your weaknesses if you don't mention mine') and needs careful boundary management and clear contracting. Hence I also specified *of equivalent status*: the power dynamics attached to

work roles mean it could be hard for a junior colleague to challenge as well as encourage a senior one. In a church or small agency, it has the advantage of supplementing scarce line management resources, with the potential for effective feedback from people who may be more closely connected in their day-to-day work than a member of a voluntary management committee. In many ways it is part of good practice for any group and a valuable tool in team ministries, for example.

Personal support
Although the personal influences the professional, in that who I am and how I am affects what I am able to do, this does not mean that the personal agenda becomes part of the responsibility of the organization. A caring management group wants to offer emotional and practical support to someone who has been bereaved, for example, but it is not their role to provide bereavement counselling. In vocational and caring roles, where the person and the role can easily become intertwined, having in place good personal support is a vital tool in preventing stress and burnout. This might take many forms, including counselling, other therapies, pastoral support or spiritual direction. It might be as simple as someone who takes on the role of key support person, making regular contact to ask 'How are you?', providing a confidential and comfortable space to listen to the answer and offering prayer and company through the walk of life. The importance of a safe space that is accessed before reaching crisis cannot be overstated.

Reflection and awareness

All these structures sound good on paper; but it takes more than the opportunity for supervision and support to be effective. The supervision meetings need to build on the ability to be a reflective practitioner (see Chapter 6), raising self-awareness and identifying strategies to deal with potential problems. It is this self-awareness, combined with an appreciation of others' vulnerability, that is the key to the safe practice of vulnerable leadership. As Mitchell writes (2003):

> Looking at Jesus we can see he was very much at home with other people's fragilities and vulnerabilities – witness his response to the Samaritan woman (John: 4) looking for love in all the wrong places. He was even in touch with his own needs and asked the disciples to connect with him during the most stressful period of his life – an invitation they neither understood nor felt comfortable with ('Peter took him aside and began to rebuke him': Mark 8.33)

Becoming transparent, to God, to self and to others is a part of the way of vulnerability that many other theologians have identified. It helps us to open ourselves to the wounding of living God's love and achieving the voluntary relinquishment of power that normally protects us (Herrick and Mann, 1998). This process of knowing ourselves, in order to empty ourselves, so we can be truly present with others and offer a love that seeks to serve rather than control, has been eloquently described by practitioners of vulnerable leadership such as Henri Nouwen and Jean Vanier (see Chapter 9). It enables us to avoid two other dangers present in pastoral and caring role relationships, namely acting out and intimacy.

Acting out

Transference is the term from the psychoanalysis field to describe the phenomena of acting out in the present the feelings and needs we had towards a significant person in the past. For example, a survivor of child abuse might unconsciously place someone providing him with pastoral support in the role of his abusive mother. He may seek an inappropriate level of intimacy and even attempt to sexualize the relationship. He may always seek approval and permission. Counter-transference occurs when the pastoral supporter fails to recognize this, and responds with a similar projection of her unmet needs onto the 'client'. Perhaps she was abused by her first husband, and projects onto the survivor her unmet needs for love and acceptance; or sometimes it may be the capacity to love herself that is impaired, so love is projected onto others. Many survivors might recognize this dynamic in their own relationships. Unrecognized, it can of course be very messy and painful. With awareness, it is just another part of our human frailty that we can accept and deal with in many ways. In client-centred therapy, the solution is seen in enabling the client to recognize himself as the source of these attitudes and feelings. It is also suggested that transference is more likely to occur when the counsellor is seen as the holder of knowledge, understanding the client better than he does himself (Rogers, 1951). In a relationship of equality and empowerment, this is avoided.

Intimacy

Like the discussion on vulnerability, I suggest that intimacy in relationships between leaders and those they serve is both a good and bad thing. It is a positive experience when it encompasses the closeness of a real encounter, person to person; where two vulnerable people can collaborate on a task, share a journey together. It is a dangerous dynamic when it is about the leaders' own needs for emotional and physical intimacy affirmation and affection, which should be met within the more equal personal relationships, with friends, spouses and families. Jesus was intimate with the disciples and all the people he was involved with in his ministry. He accepted their love and care without exclusion;

but his ultimate source of love and support was the triune God of his being. I can't help thinking that in one sense, that means he loved himself. So it is in the fusion of a lifelong committed relationship, such as marriage, that we experience the self-loving of trinity and the God of love.

Boundaries

This ability to distinguish appropriately between personal and professional boundaries is another vital skill in safe practice. For someone new and inexperienced in leadership, particularly, being able to recognize, draw and maintain clear boundaries of role, agenda, and attachment is a core skill. Boundaries provide safety and security and also freedom. A child who can be trusted not to stray out of sight is allowed to play freely in the park. She is happy not to keep testing that boundary because she has learnt to trust it will give her that freedom. A child who has been ignored one minute, then told off for running away the next, learns not to trust, not to take responsibility for herself and probably ends up confined to the pushchair.

Clarifying the boundaries
In both individual and group relationships, we need to practise establishing an agreement or 'contract' that ensures a shared understanding of what these boundaries are. It should clarify:

- what are the rights and responsibilities implied in the relationships
- what are the 'rules' including confidentiality
- how the responsibility for maintaining the boundary is shared (recognizing the power dynamic)
- what are the practical boundaries of task, environment, agenda, timing and so on
- what happens if someone is uncomfortable or feels that a boundary has been violated or broken

Pushing the boundaries
It is important to be aware of the potential for both enrichment and confusion or conflict of having unclear boundaries, and particularly of holding more than one role boundary with someone. For example, being a wife and a supervisor, a counsellor and a friend, a minister and a line manager, can create role confusion. Again it is partly about inequality and partly about emotional projection. If you (my minister) have to address some critical feedback with me as my line manager, I can hear behind it the greater spiritual weight of my minister – and end up feeling resentful. I feel I've experienced too much of God's anger and not enough of his love! On the other hand, a counsellor who risks crossing the boundary of friendship, can rekindle the capacity to love in

community of someone who was not able to break out of their isolation on their own. Stretching boundaries is risky and must be monitored through rigorous supervision. It is also a skill to develop slowly and carefully, based on increasing experience. But I am with the school of thought that says we are to act professionally and also prophetically; and that as Christ broke the rules and engaged passionately with life, so should we when God demands it. I don't believe that rigid boundaries and professional distance are adequate to encourage the wild love that is the wild hope of the gospel.

Power-sharing

In Chapter 3 I talked about the holding of power on behalf of the community and suggested that it is the application rather than the location that we should concentrate on. In youth work, the processes of empowerment and participation are recognized as both the goals and the methodology at the heart of good practice: 'The underpinning principles of all youth work, including that with young people who are disadvantaged and marginalized, are the same. Youth work is empowering and educative, strives to offer equality of opportunity and works to encourage young people's fuller participation' (DfEE/NYA, 2000). The exercise of leadership that releases rather than holds on to power, collaborates rather than rescues, also promotes a non-abusive culture. There are a number of arenas of good practice that can provide tools and models for increasing participation and developing collaborative practice.

1   **Social capital** is a relatively recently developed concept that examines and values the 'connections among individuals – social networks and the norms of reciprocity and trustworthiness that arise from them' (Putnam, 2000). This concept gives value to relationships and mutuality rather than resources and winners, echoing the gospel priorities.
2   **Anti-oppressive practice** is perhaps another term to describe a non-abusive culture that actively challenges abuse where it is acknowledged. There is an established history of anti-racist, anti-sexist work that recognizes the need not just to empower individuals, but also change the culture that maintains the abuse.

> What our work with these young black disabled women and men showed was that independence was not just about doing things themselves, but having the opportunity to have an input into what affects their lives. They said independence is about having choice and control. However, family and cultural expectations often affected their ability to exercise this choice. (Bignall, 2000, p. 21)

3 **Participation.** Youth work and radical community work both bring
  long experience of participation and community governance. True
  participation is about more than token gestures to bring outside
  voices into our structures (e.g. two youth places on a church
  council). It is more than setting up a parallel structure that creates
  inequality and can impede dialogue (e.g. a youth council run on
  similar lines to the main council and with a token budget). It is
  about growing real governance within the community of outsiders,
  tackling the power structures on their ground, being prepared to
  dismantle the old models and exercise real power through the new
  (such as a web-based youth forum that has been modelled on the
  lessons and experienced gained with a group of young people
  designing and negotiating their own local skatepark).

Rest and play

It has already been noted how work isn't everything. Yet within
Christian service and ministry, sometimes it can feel like it is. Job descriptions, supervision and clear boundaries should help to avoid the
workaholic or work-overload scenarios that are unhealthy for both the
individual and those they work with. When it comes to time for rest and
play, there are other people to be considered too! Our families and
friends, especially partners, spouses and children, deserve to be with us
in our play not just our recuperation. Good management takes care to
protect the health of the family as well as the individual, and that means
ensuring that the organization is not heaping too many expectations on
one person's shoulders. It is why the model of collaborative ministry, far
from being the threat that some people used to one-man-bands thought
it would be, in fact liberates everyone to be themselves and have their
own space. Sometimes, particularly for the families of those in full-time
ministry and service, the boundaries between work and home can
become increasingly blurred and home life can lose out. For others, the
energy and focus of the work becomes the centre of life, pulling attention
and love away from the family, and difficult emotions arise. These kinds
of scenarios are not uncommon in the stories of church leaders who
abuse. Research with Anglican clergy about the causes of sexual misconduct identified stress, loneliness and neediness as major factors (Birchard,
2000). It is a real priority to put attention and resources into family
support for ministers, youth workers, counsellors and others whose
vocation to caring can easily take over their home and relationships.

Prayer

I have left prayer until last not because it is least important – in fact I
am one of those people who always saves the best until last! It is of

course the beginning and the end of everything we do and if I have not appeared to talk about it more within this volume, it is because of two assumptions that I make:

1   Because I am writing particularly for a Christian audience, I don't need to lecture you about regular prayer.
2   In my understanding, this whole book is a prayer because it describes a continuing conversation with God.

This conversation is the most vital feature of our best practice. At a Radical Journey event in 2002, Jim Wallis pointed out it is 'moral authority not power that has the capacity to bring change, and this comes through times of spiritual preparation'. As individuals and as organizations, our spiritual development should be built on an engagement in worship that allows us the experience of vulnerability in the safety of God's house. Jean Vanier (1989) describes this non-abusive community as one founded on love:

> Love makes us weak and vulnerable because it breaks down the barriers and protective armour we have built around ourselves. Love means letting others reach us and being sensitive enough to reach them. The cement of unity is interdependence . . . community is made by the gentle concern that people show each other every day.

DISCUSSION QUESTIONS

To discuss
Have you ever experienced abuse of power by someone in authority? What do you think are the qualities of good leadership? What practices are most important to ensure power is not abused?

To reflect
At the end of the chapter, I suggest spiritual preparation is at the heart of good practice. What else can you do to develop your spiritual life? When are you vulnerable with God?

To do
The quote from Jean Vanier talks about the 'gentle concern that people show each other every day' (see above). Often that is in the little things: making someone a cup of tea, calling to see if they are all right, offering to help with the daily chores, giving a bunch of flowers. Perhaps you could make an extra effort to make your concern for your friends and neighbours real, today and tomorrow, until it becomes a habit.

References

Adirondack, S., *Just about Managing? Effective management for voluntary organizations and community groups*, London Voluntary Service Council, London, 1998.

Bignall, T., in *Young People Now*, August 2000.

Birchard, T., 'Clergy sexual misconduct: frequency and causation', *Sexual and Relationship Therapy*, 15 February 2000.

Bonhoeffer, D., *Letters and Papers from Prison* (enlarged edn), SCM Press, London, 1971.

Broadbent, J., 'Non-Managerial Supervision: An Overview' in Marken, M. and Payne, M. (eds), *Enabling and Ensuring: Supervision in Practice*, National Youth Bureau/Council for Education and Training in Youth and Community Work, Leicester, 1987.

Community Education Service, 'Step by Step Staff Development Scheme', Suffolk County Council, 1993.

Department for Education and Employment/National Youth Association, *Moving on Up: how youth work raises achievement and promotes social inclusion*, DfEE/NYA, London, 2000.

Herrick, V. and Mann, I., *Jesus Wept: Reflections on Vulnerability in Leadership*, Darton, Longman & Todd, London, 1998.

Mitchell, R., 'Sexual Abuse – Helping to Heal', *The Church of England Newspaper*, 23 October 2003.

Putnam, R. D., *Bowling Alone. The collapse and revival of American community*, Simon and Schuster, New York, 2000.

Rogers, C., *Client-Centered Therapy*, Constable & Co., London, 1951.

Time for Action: Sexual abuse, the Churches and a new dawn for survivors, The Report to Churches Together in Britain and Ireland of the Group established to examine issues of Sexual Abuse, Churches Together in Britain and Ireland, London, 2002.

Vanier, J., *Community and Growth*, Darton, Longman & Todd, London, 1989.

8

Safer Communities:
best practice in specific contexts

———◄○►———

Or maybe the purpose of being here, wherever we are, is to increase the
durability and the occasions of love among and between peoples. Love,
as the concentration of tender caring and tender excitement, or love as
the reason for joy . . . Love is the single true prosperity of any moment
and that whatever and whoever impedes, diminishes, ridicules, opposes
the development of loving spirit is 'wrong'/hateful.

Jordan, 1983

I once asked a colleague on the youth ministry degree course, what he
hoped to achieve over the three years with the students we taught. His
instinctive response was, 'for them to know they are loved'.[1] In the
many following discussions about educational approaches, value for
money, targets and outcomes, assessment, personal and professional
formation and all the other preoccupations of higher education and professional and ministerial formation, I tried to hold on to that aphorism.
If God's purpose and being are Love, and my mission is to share in
God's mission, then all that I do should be love. I frequently need to
remind myself to check my actions and behaviour against this principle,
and I often find I have not been as loving as I could, and sometimes
quite unloving! But it makes sense to me in my heart and in my head
that love is my calling and response, in the detail of life as much as in
the vision.

When we embarked on a round of child protection training with
voluntary youth and children's leaders in the rural diocese I worked in
ten years ago, some of the proposals felt quite threatening to smaller
churches. We were promoting taking up references, always having two
leaders, not taking children home in the car on your own. People
objected that this would put volunteers off and was just unrealistic in a
rural community; you couldn't get two leaders, parents didn't collect
their children, the work would have to shut down and it was all our

fault. I both understood and sympathized with this response. It is even harder now than ever to recruit regular leaders, and transport is always an issue. However, I also challenged us to think about it as an opportunity not a threat. As a parent, I would say, I want my child to have the very best of everything. I want him to be safe, nurtured and to grow in body, mind and spirit. I don't want him to hear the gospel stuck in a cold and dusty vestry with an isolated leader who is profoundly committed, but also unsupported, under-resourced and probably lacking in spiritual nourishment herself, as she hasn't had a break from teaching the children for weeks. (I know what that's like – I've been there!) I would rather we closed the children's group, if that's the best we can do. Better for him to stay with me in church, in a community of all-age pilgrims, who can witness to the joys and struggles of life as God's gathered community, bringing our praise and fears from our homes and places of work, living the rhythm of the gospel through the passing of the church year, singing, praying and learning together to the best of our ability. At least there is a community sharing that task, and if we have to work a little at including different needs in our gathered times, as least there are plenty of us to lend ideas and energy.

So this chapter is aimed at achieving the best practice possible in some of the main areas of working with people of all ages in our communities. This is not to expect perfection; but in accepting the idea of doing something well enough, I believe it is important not to set the standard for deciding what is 'good enough' too low. However, it is also necessary to devise strategies that are achievable. Many organizations and churches now have child protection policies and procedures and most offer training to paid and voluntary staff. It is my experience that sometimes this guidance is not implemented fully, because it is unrealistic or it isn't given sufficient priority, time and resources. I want to promote good enough solutions which balance the agreed principles with the realism of working within the voluntary sector. I also want to argue that this needs to be an area of priority, not just within churches, but all organizations and communities that are vulnerable to abuse.

What follows are practical guidelines for working with people of all ages in most situations. Much of the guidance applicable to youth and children's work is also sensible when working with adults, particularly 'vulnerable' adults. This definition could include many of us at particular times in our lives: we may be vulnerable due to physical or learning disability, age, mental distress, bereavement, family break-up, debilitating illness or simply the stress and overload of daily life. So I suggest that most of the ideas about best practice from the youth work field that I normally teach, can be translated into good practice for inclusive and non-abusive work with people in any context. Space precludes dealing with any particular issues that arise from particular contexts, such as work with children, young people and families; pastoral care, and counselling or healing/prayer ministry. See Chapter 10 for suggested resources in these areas.

Regulation and information

The first task is to ensure there are clear guidelines for every area of work we are involved in. These may be prescribed by national bodies or suggested by organizations with particular expertise. If you need to create your own, it is always better to seek advice from others who have relevant experience and knowledge, to avoid re-inventing the wheel and making serious mistakes due to ignorance. It is always possible to adapt material sensibly to your specific context; this is far easier than dealing with the consequences of a crisis that may have been avoided. There are many good resource agencies listed in Chapter 10.

Policies

These are more likely to get read and implemented if they are as short, clear and simple as possible. A policy statement should make the intention of the organization clear and the principles any practice will be based on. It is likely to include:

1 A statement of intent, e.g. 'This organization is committed to providing the best possible level of care, protection and support to the children and young people we work with.'
2 Core principles for practice, e.g. 'We will ensure all our work is undertaken to the standards recommended by the government, our national body and the professional best practice of the field.' This may also refer to any relevant ethical code or code of conduct.
3 Theological principles (in Christian contexts), e.g. 'This policy is founded on our belief in the intrinsic value of each individual as a child of God, and expresses our Christian calling to nurture the young and protect the vulnerable.' This may also refer to any mission statement or statement of beliefs.
4 Identification of all procedures and guidelines attached to the policy.
5 Any other implementation information, e.g. the date the policy was adopted, date of review, person/body responsible for implementation and monitoring, contact details.

Procedures

These provide the detail of how the policy will be implemented. They should only include the minimum information necessary, or people won't remember and therefore can't implement them. The following points can assist implementation:

1 Consider providing different levels of information to different people; for example, a member needs to know who to complain to, a volunteer may only need to know how to pass on a concern or complaint, those with management responsibility need guidance on how to handle complaints that are received.

2 Ensure set procedures describe what *must* happen in a particular set of circumstances, e.g. if abuse is expected or disclosed. Everyone is expected to follow these at all times and they must be very clear and precise.

3 Rules or standards are also required to be met by everyone, for example minimum staff ratios. They are not areas likely to be adapted to different situations or open to discretion.

4 Guidelines indicate what the organization considers to be the best course to follow in general practice and in some specific situations. It may not be possible to cover every eventuality; hence these are guidelines not simple rules. It is wise to include all the common situations anyone in your organization is likely to face. It can be helpful to affirm to staff that in other situations they are encouraged to use their judgement to respond, within the principles described in the policy. This can be written into the guidelines and talked through during training.

Ownership

A policy is more likely to be implemented effectively if everyone understands what it means, has a stake in it and trusts the process. There are several ways to support such ownership.

1 The best place to start is at the beginning. When creating or reviewing major policies and procedures, identify the key stakeholders and involve them in the process, whether through open consultation or inviting people to join the writing group. This is a good opportunity to give space to the voices that are often hidden or ignored when such documents are written. For example, a family centre might invite representatives from management, paid and volunteer staff, parents, children, and key agencies such as Social Services or Home Start.

2 The same range of voices should be included in monitoring and review procedures. It is good to get a range of experience; continuing the above example, it might mean asking a family who used to use the centre, another who is a long-standing user and one who has just started coming. Finding appropriate ways to consult is also important. Not everyone can contribute equally in a formal meeting structure, but most of us will respond to an informal 'interview' over

a cup of tea. Some people love completing questionnaires. Children may prefer to draw 'what I like about here' or 'my ideal family centre'.

3 Once you have guidelines, everyone needs to know about them. Staff and managers will need training. Anyone affected (parents, children and young people, clients, members, supporters) need to know about it and how to access those parts that affect them. Not only does it make the words in the policy real, it also increases transparency and helps people to trust the organization. Adult survivors of abuse, for example, will feel safer in a church where they know what will happen with any offender who joins the congregation. Governing bodies and national structures you are a part of may require a copy of the policy to be lodged with them. You can increase trust and inter-agency relationships by informing agencies you regularly network with. User-friendly summaries are particularly useful for distribution to a wider range of stakeholders.

Training

It may sound obvious to say that all the time and energy put into producing guidelines for best practice will be wasted without an equal investment in training, but I often meet people, especially volunteers, who receive little or no training for what they do. I consider it a good rule of thumb to put at least 10 per cent of an organization's resources into training. This might be measured by time as much as finance, for example a volunteer working one session a week for say 40 weeks of the year, could be offered four sessions of training per annum. By training I mean equipping people for the role they are undertaking, enabling them to grow and learn through the job, and to update their skills and knowledge with their peers. This very rarely includes telling people what to do in a disempowering way!

Induction

I am assuming that everyone appointed to a role has been through an appropriate appointment process (see later section) and has a clear job description and supervision and support arrangements (see Chapter 7). A well-managed induction process, which might include any trial or probationary period, is sound investment. It should provide the main information anyone needs at the start of a new position in order to fulfil their responsibilities. It also ensures they have the support to overcome any initial lack of confidence or experience and helps to establish identity as part of a team or wider organization. This is the time to include familiarization with the most important polices and guidelines the person will need in their post.

Practice

This isn't intended to be a training manual, but if I were to be asked what are the three most important lessons I have learnt from training with people on best practice, these would be top of the list:

1 It really helps to start where people are. If our existing knowledge and experience is affirmed, we feel more confident that we can move into areas that may be new to us. If we understand why we need to do something in a certain way, we are probably more likely to do it.

2 It is important that written guidelines become living things not dead documents. It helps to introduce the policy in the context of a training session, not just telling people to read a large pile of paperwork (although some people might appreciate the chance to read it beforehand so they can digest it and prepare any questions; others won't bother!). A well-structured session might cover the background to the policy, familiarizing people with what it contains, checking that it is understood and providing an opportunity for questions and any issues they might raise. But the most important element is *application*. Give plenty of opportunity for the group to practise applying the policy to typical scenarios they might come across in their work.

3 Empowerment is a principle that applies to training as much as leadership and other areas of work. To me this has many implications; recognizing that I am not an expert and everyone in the group will contribute so we learn together what best practice might look like; helping people to discover their own solutions rather than imposing my own; making sure the quietest voices have an opportunity to be heard; modelling the non-abusive good practice we are trying to develop in the training sessions themselves.

Review

The best training happens within a thought-out staff development policy. This will include supervision to provide accountability and support and help us to identify training needs. Particularly when new procedures are introduced, it is important to log who has attended the accompanying training and to provide them with an attendance certificate or some evidence of what they have covered. Regular updates are important as our practice develops and ideas change. Training should be personalized in the sense that you should follow a programme that addresses areas of weakness where those are essential to fulfil the role; but also develop areas of strength as these are likely to be the gifts you have been called to use and where you will be most motivated and successful.

Transparency and safety

The detail of most good practice is easy to work out once you have grasped the basic principles of working openly (abuse feeds off a culture of secrecy); with accountability (so others have oversight of what you are doing); and with adequate personnel and resources to do the job well and have enough capacity spare to cope when things go wrong. The key areas of best practice below all follow these principles; some of the thinking has developed out of work with children and young people but applies just as well to any age group.

Recruitment and appointment

Advertising both paid and voluntary posts brings the trust of an open process and gives a more equal opportunity for new people to become involved in leadership roles. A trial period, during which time the person is under the supervision of an 'approved' leader, enables both the organization and the new recruit to check that this really is the right role for them. Criminal Record Bureau (CRB) background checks should be carried out at the appropriate level for anyone working with children, young people or vulnerable adults; this has to happen through a registered body (see Resources section). Just as important is a proper appointment procedure, including an interview and taking up background and character references. Once the interview, CRB check and references, and any probationary period have been satisfactory completed, the person can be designated an 'approved' leader; until then they should be supervised.

Staffing levels

As a general rule there should always be at least two leaders for any activity to run. At least one of these must be an approved leader. I prefer to try to keep this rule even when, say, running a training group with adults; although not essential in that situation, it models good practice and enables peer feedback. I would certainly require two leaders for any group working with vulnerable adults, as well as youth and children's work. (See the resources section for ratios for children's groups.) Where it is necessary to break up into smaller groups, perhaps to keep the age-range down in Sunday groups for children, transparency can be maintained with only one leader if they are in shared rooms or adjoining each other; and it is the practice for another approved leader to visit regularly. It is not just safety that is increased by this rule. Having leaders of different ages, genders and personalities working together creates an openness and range of relationship and working styles that makes the group more inclusive for the variety of people who are members.

One-to-one

Generally the only context when leaders should meet someone on their own is when it is essential to the role, they are appropriately trained to do so and are receiving professional supervision (e.g. an accredited counseller).

One-to-one situations between a leader and any vulnerable person should be avoided, except where pastoral reasons, a person's request, or immediate group safety demand an extra degree of confidentiality. In these cases another approved adult should be made aware of the situation and be within easy reach of the meeting. It is best if the door of the room where the adult and person are meeting is left ajar. Where possible a corner of the group activity room or a room with a window in the door should be used (so the conversation is overlooked). If the person should become distressed during the meeting then the adult should resist the desire to give physical comfort unless requested by the person concerned (see the safe touch guidelines). If touching does occur in a one-to-one situation then another approved adult must be informed as soon as possible, and if it is felt necessary then the supervisor should also be informed.

For ministers and others involved in pastoral care and used to the traditional model of visiting people at home, this is not as difficult as it might first seem. It provides an opportunity to create some clearer boundaries around professional and personal relationships. The formation of pastoral teams means essential visiting can be done in pairs, or when it is known that other members of a household will also be around. A working space can be defined, like a side room or vicarage study, and used so that it creates safety for the person seeking the meeting. For example, I offer students I supervise the choice of meeting in a town café (a public space) or in my home. If they want the peace of the latter, I try to make sure it is at a time when my husband or grown-up children may be around for at least part of the time – there is the safety of knowing we will be 'interrupted'. This helps us to think of more creative ways to meet people's pastoral needs; rather than a home visit, encouraging an isolated single parent to attend a pram service, or helping with baby-sitting so they can join a house group, might be a better solution.

Transport

No leader should ever travel alone with a vulnerable person of any age. There are several ways to achieve this. Friends and parents can be encouraged to transport their own friends and family, where they are not able to get somewhere under their own steam. Two leaders can share a car or minibus together. I think it is reasonable in rural areas, where public transport is limited, for a single leader to transport a group by car where there is no other alternative. This should be the occasional exception rather than normal practice, and should be logged. Also it should be arranged so that the last pair are dropped off together. Practice should ensure that the timings of journeys are logged. This catches out, for example, the abuser who stops at the garage on the way home for an ice-cream, then pulls into a quiet lay-by.

Managing risk

All organizations should undertake a comprehensive risk assessment that covers all aspects of their work. This includes, but is not limited to, health and safety. Resources, reputation and goals all face risks which can prevent us from achieving our mission. Harm may be caused to us, colleagues and partners or the general public. The idea of risk management is not necessarily to remove the risk but to reduce its adverse impact. For example, I am a keen sailor and the biggest risk factors are the engine, the weather and human error. The first is pretty essential, the second uncontrollable and the third is not preventable! But I can reduce the potential harmful impact through training, planning, maintenance and safe practices such as always wearing harnesses (it is easier to fall in the water than get out of it!). Some of the risk areas it is wise to consider are those covered by legislation, where it is important to get the correct advice and keep policies and practice up to date.

1 *Health and safety* is one such key area. There is a lot of free advice and resource material available from the Health and Safety Executive. The main points to consider are risk assessment regarding hazards from buildings, working practices and potentially hazardous substances (such as cleaning materials). Generally sensible precautions are enough, but doing nothing will be considered negligent if there is a hazardous incident.
2 *Food hygiene* is another area that can catch out voluntary organizations. Both venue and personnel need to be up to correct standards when handling anything other than pre-packaged food (such as chocolate bars.) Again, there is free advice available and easy access to basic training. Local environmental health offices are the first point of contact.
3 *First aid* can be overlooked, as most of the regulations come in for businesses employing over a certain number of people, and smaller organizations may not reach that threshold. Youth work is often in that situation, but I always recommend that people follow the basic level of safe practice anyway. It is necessary to have a procedure for logging and reporting any incidents; and this can help to notice a pattern of unexplained injuries in the context of suspected physical abuse. I also believe every group activity should have someone present with at least a basic level of first-aid training; more if the risks are higher, such as sports. Both St John Ambulance and the Red

Cross provide training, equipment and advice; and for larger events (such as concerts, fetes, tournaments, etc.) it is worth considering boosting your first-aid team by engaging their services.

4   *Data protection* is the other major risk area covered by legislation. Again the government website contains much helpful information. Many charities that only use the information for their own records, such as membership lists, do not need to register – beware of expensive scams that are posing as the data protection agency threatening legal action if you don't register with them. However, you still need to comply with good practice, especially regarding safe storage of information, permission to hold records and an individual's access to any information held about them.

5   *Fire safety* is the final area to mention in this overview. Premises should be inspected and have adequate fire-safety equipment, which must be regularly checked and maintained. Both staff and building users should practise evacuation techniques; if there is no requirement set down by your size and public usage, I suggest termly is a safe practice. If you hold public events such as concerts, you will probably need a Public Entertainments Licence (contact your local council), which will specify the number of people etc. and also covers health and safety and noise. Other licences or permissions will more than likely be required for any of the following activities: broadcasting live or recorded music; recording music; performing music or plays that another person or body holds copyright to; copying the words or score of any musical item; copying any published material (such as worship material or book extracts); showing films or videos or receiving TV broadcasts. Your local association of voluntary organizations is a good place to start if you need further information and advice.

Listening and respect

We have seen how abusive leadership thrives on secrecy and unchallenged power; a careful listening culture is a fundamental principle that avoids such dangers. Listening to the most quiet and vulnerable in our communities requires some thought and effort. Coming at the issue from the other end, treating all people with the same respect and empowering them to take responsibility for themselves has a similar positive outcome. You learn to respect my space and I learn to say 'No' if you get uncomfortably near.

Creating a listening culture

Telling people they are important to us holds more truth if we show them they have value in our attitudes and actions towards them. This means involving them in decisions that affect them; giving them space to express their needs and desires and ensuring these shape our response; valuing their contribution and hearing their story. All this involves being good listeners more than being good talkers or doers. I listen well when I suspend my own needs, activity and agenda for a while to create space to concentrate on yours. I am not listening if I am already framing my response while you are telling me your story; or butting in with empathetic examples of when I experienced something similar (because of course that was my experience, which was different from yours). I listen well when I understand the barriers that prevent you from sharing easily, and try to create a safe space for you to share. I listen well when I check out with you that I have understood correctly, avoid rushing in with my solutions, accompany you on the journey you have chosen and wait for you to finish before I respond. I don't listen well when I think that I have all the answers already, that I know what you're going to say before you say it, that I know better than you or that what you have to say is not worth hearing. A listening culture is one that creates space for everyone to contribute, waits for them to finish speaking and is shaped by their perspectives. This is vulnerable leadership based on trust and empowerment.

Listening well

It may take some enlightened reviewing to identify our strengths and weaknesses as listeners, and some creative thinking to work out how to improve. Asking the questions: 'Who are the voiceless people in our community?' and 'Where do we go to hear what they have to say?' can produce some surprising answers.

1　Sometimes we can make assumptions about people's ability to contribute. I was a member of a group in an Anglican diocese that wanted to consider the practice of children receiving communion before they are confirmed, which had already been experimented with in some parishes. We could have set up a committee of adults to evaluate the parishes' experience and write a new policy. Instead we held a workshop, bringing together children, parents, church leaders and clergy to share and debate together. We divided up into peer groups to share stories, issues and ideas. An interesting range of perspectives emerged. Clergy and leaders were particularly concerned with theological issues, how much the children understood, and how to ensure a parish was united behind any new practice introduced. They highlighted how teaching the children about communion also helped to refresh the adults' understanding! Parents were generally keen to identify the benefits of including their children, and to review preparation and teaching material that would continue to disciple the children. The children, from as young as two or three, were very clear and matter-of-fact. They drew

pictures and told stories that demonstrated they understood enough
and had their own views: 'This bread is Jesus' body. This wine is
Jesus' blood. 'Cos he died for us.' 'I like the taste of real bread. I
don't like the wafers. The wine tastes funny.' 'Before we were left out
and just got a pat on the head. Now I feel part of Jesus' body, the
same as everyone else.' They also had lots of constructive criticism
to offer about the teaching materials. I'm sure all these voices made
a significant impact on the shape of the final policy.

2 Sometimes we need to make an extra effort to ensure people are able
to use their voice. In children's work, it is a growing practice to
identify someone who is outside the normal leadership to be an independent listener. This person is available for the children to talk to
if they have any concerns they are uncomfortable about sharing with
the regular leaders. Their role is to listen to the children, respond
appropriately and act as an advocate for them, over child protection,
bullying, harassment or other serious issues affecting their well-
being. Their task is to listen to the children's experience and
concerns, to as far as possible respond as the child requests, but
always ensuring that the welfare of the child comes first. The person
chosen will normally be someone with some experience and training
in counselling, mentoring or advocacy work. Steps are taken to
introduce them to the children and ensure they are accessible to
them directly, perhaps through a regular visit, a letter box, a phone
number. It is made clear that the independent listener practises
confidentiality, with the normal arrangements for reporting chid
protection issues. I think a similar role could be very helpful in many
other organizations and churches; someone who is not in the
leadership or on the managing body, but who is able to act
independently, for example if concerns are raised about the leadership of the organization. Maybe someone who is tasked to seek out
the voices that aren't normally heard, and create time and space to
listen to them.

3 Sometimes creating a comfortable context for listening helps us to be
better listeners. In recent years, organizations concerned with the
family have promoted the idea of reviving the family meal, whether
daily or a few times a week, without the distraction of TV, as a time
to talk and listen to each other. A meal can be a great informal and
relaxed time to share in equal fellowship, as modelled by Jesus
throughout his ministry and relived each time we break bread in his
name. I'm sure the success of initiatives like Alpha rests as much on
the meal as on the Word; God is in the midst of the supper and, like
us, is using that time to listen to everyone's stories.

4 Sometimes we need to reach outside our organizations to hear those
vital forgotten voices, not just open our doors, issue an invitation
and expect them to walk in. This was certainly Jesus' model: he went

to the people and didn't wait for an invitation! Staff from a building-based youth project, for example, might undertake outreach work with young people on the streets, in schools or local meeting places, to discover what they think of the project, any reasons why they don't use it, what are their wants and needs. It is the basics of mission: we need to talk to the people who haven't yet joined the conversation even more than those who already have.

Respect

It sounds obvious to say that non-abusive practice must be founded on treating people with respect, and asking the same from them. Yet when I evaluate my practice, I discover that isn't always as easy as it sounds. Sometimes I am too focused on my own agenda, or too caught up in strong emotions to treat everyone with the same respect. Sometimes politeness and the habit of saying 'yes' more than 'no' means I allow people to take advantage of me or accept their abuse silently and passively.

1 I think respect means giving space to other people and their agendas, recognizing they are no more or less important than me. Jesus demonstrated this all the time in the way he treated people. He gave time to the unrespectable, and argued with the leadership. He ignored Herod and placed a child in the middle. It can take a conscious effort to give that space and value to everyone. The way we include children in worship is a good example. With the best intentions, we ask them to contribute to a service, but on our terms; we want them to sing at a particular point, for example, and we choose the song. More respectful to them, and less restricting of the ministry God calls them to, would be to explore the theme of the service with them and seek their ideas, allowing their authentic voice to come through in their contribution. Most of the best worship I have participated in has emerged from this kind of respect.

2 Respecting boundaries is another key area. We need to develop good awareness of each other's personal space, and not invade it. The practice of safe touch is based on this principle. Any touching between a leader and someone they are serving should take place in public. Touching should be age-appropriate and initiated by the person being worked with rather than by the leader. Touching should be related to the person's needs rather than the leader's. Leaders must always avoid any physical activity that may have sexual overtones. We are all entitled to determine the degree of physical contact we have with others, except when there is significant risk to ourselves or others (for example, if a fight breaks out), or our capacity to consent is temporarily impaired but may reasonably be assumed (for example, I am unconscious and need urgent

resuscitation). No leader should use physical discipline with anyone at any time. Safe 'holding' may only be used in extreme circumstances where there is immediate danger of personal injury to the person being restrained or another person, and should be undertaken by someone suitably trained. Physical care assistance for children and disabled people who require it should be at their request, appropriate to their age and disability and carried out by approved leaders who have been trained. Respecting these touch boundaries is very important with adults who have been abused. You may think it's friendly to bound up behind me and give me a hug; I may experience it as a flashback to physical abuse, triggering very bad emotions and reliving the events, or an embarrassing defensive response that could involve turning round and hitting you away! You may think I'm unfriendly because I don't greet people with a hug or a handshake; I may simply not be ready to trust touching another person yet, as a result of sexual abuse that violated all my touch boundaries. On the other hand, it is acceptable and I think important that if I ask for a hug when I am upset, you feel able to give one if you are happy to. (See chapter 5.)

3   Self-respect is an equal partner to respecting others. We all need to learn to hold our boundaries clearly, to say 'no' to something that is unacceptable or makes us feel uncomfortable, and to ask for what we need. This doesn't mean it becomes our responsibility to stop people abusing us – primarily it is their responsibility not to do it! But it does help us to be less vulnerable. We need to foster a culture where 'no' is allowed as well as 'yes', where people aren't pressurized into doing things they really don't want to by subtle means such as questioning their commitment, motivation or judgement in saying no. How many times have you genuinely affirmed someone who has made a refusal, compared to the number of times you have rewarded acceptance? We should help children and adults to recognize their own boundaries, know they have a right to be respected and to develop the assertiveness to state and hold their personal space.

Empowering relationships

Laughter and joy

If we are safe from abusive relationships through these practices, what are we safe for? McCarty (1996) suggests the qualities below are key to healthy relationships and should be what we model and teach. Most of these have been explored already, but perhaps the last deserves a mention. I am convinced that the human capacity for humour is a God-given quality that comes from the belly of the Supreme Being! The wisdom of the fool has long recognized that comedy and tragedy are two sides of the same face, and the psalms proclaim this: 'those who

sow in tears will reap with songs of joy' (Psalm 126.5). In the seriousness of tackling abuse, let us not lose our capacity to laugh with the
absurdities of existence, recapturing the sheer joy in life itself that is an
innocent child's and benefiting from its healing properties. So I suggest
the following qualities of joyfulness:

- open communication
- appropriate affection
- honesty and forgiveness
- vulnerability
- dependability
- freedom
- patience
- humour

Education

We do most of our learning about relationships through experience.
Friendship doesn't occupy a large space in the school curriculum and
there aren't many adult evening classes on the subject. Even Christian
teaching can appear to have a higher concern for the morality of our
relationships than for learning which helps create positive and non-
abusive associations and friendships. Yet relating to God in community,
a God who is relationship (in the Trinity), is the heart of our faith and
one way of understanding our mission. A society that gave more time
and resources to education for positive relationships, based on the
qualities of joyfulness listed above, could make a significant impact on
the prevalence of abuse and its messy consequences. This view is also
borne out by research within specific abuse areas. For example,
Mullender (2000), writing about domestic violence, calls for primary
prevention work with children and young people that raises awareness
and influences attitudes and behaviour; and secondary prevention work
with men who abuse that tackles parenting skills as well as violent
behaviour. There are good models to build on in a number of fields:
parenting classes and family centres; assertiveness training and anger
management; personal, social and health education in schools and
youth organizations.

Empowerment

I hope that everything else I have written in this book points to my
fundamental belief in a God who empowers rather than rescues, and
expects us to strive to treat others the same way. God didn't just pluck
the Chosen People out of the slavery of Egypt, but encouraged,
equipped and empowered them to march out themselves on a long and
challenging journey. In theology, it is this connection of free will with
unconditional love, which forgives and redeems my mistakes, but

allows me to rejoice in my own achievements. In practice, I have found the concepts of transactional analysis particularly helpful in working out how to empower rather than rescue, persecute or stay as victim. Napper and Newton (2000) suggests an empowering style requires being responsive, vulnerable and authentic, all autonomous behaviours. I am neither taking away your power nor giving you mine. In affirming my own integrity, I release you to occupy your true shape, with the encouragement and acceptance of the father to the prodigal son. In youth work we talk a lot about building positive self-esteem, as an empowerment goal. I see that as a loving journey of shared discovery: 'Nothing you become will disappoint me; I have no preconception that I'd like to see you be or do. I have no desire to foresee you, only to discover you. You can't disappoint me' (Haskell in Schutz and Hoffman, 1975, p. 11).

DISCUSSION QUESTIONS

To discuss

What do you think about all the current activity aimed at protecting children and vulnerable people? Do you embrace it as good practice or despair at bureaucracy gone mad? What do you think are the keys to protecting the vulnerable?

To reflect

Do you agree that empowerment is preferable to rescue? How does God encourage, equip and empower you? Read the final quote of the chapter aloud and imagine God is saying that to you particularly. How does it feel to be discovered?

To do

What does it mean to you to give and receive respect? Perhaps you can review your own interpersonal relationships in this regard. If you are involved in any work with children or young people, or vulnerable adults, you could identify the strengths and weaknesses in your practice and strategies for any changes you consider necessary.

Notes

1   Revd Dr Bob Mayo, Director of the Centre for Youth Ministry, Ridley Hall, Cambridge.

References

Dante, T., with Fisher, J., *Our Little Secret: my life in the shadow of abuse*, Hodder & Stoughton, London, 2001.

Haskell, M., in *I care about your happiness: quotations from the love letters of Kahlil Gibran and Mary Haskell* selected by Schutz, S. and Hoffman, N., designed by Schutz, Dr S., Blue Mountain Arts, Colorado & Continental Publications, 1975 (Athena International edn, 1977).

Jordan, J., in *Home Girls: A Black Feminist Anthology*, ed. Smith, B., Kitchen Table: Women of Colour Press, New York, 1983.

McCarty, R., *Teen to Teen: Responding to Peers in Crisis*, St Mary's Press, Winona, MN, 1996.

Mullender, A., *Reducing Domestic Violence . . . what works? Meeting the needs of children*, Crime Reduction Research Series, Policing and Reducing Crime Unit, London, 2000.

Napper, R. and Newton, T., *Tactics: transactional analysis concepts for all trainers, teachers and tutors, plus insight into collaborative learning strategies*, TA Resources, Ipswich, 2000.

9

Relinquishment and Reshaping: towards a survivors' theology

————◄○►————

Before they had gone to bed, all the men from every part of the city of Sodom – both young and old – surrounded the house. They called to Lot, 'Where are the men who came to you tonight? Bring them out to us so that we can have sex with them.'

Lot went outside to meet them and shut the door behind him and said, 'No, my friends. Don't do this wicked thing. Look, I have two daughters who have never slept with a man. Let me bring them out to you, and you can do what you like with them.'

Genesis 19.4–8

Wrestling with angels

As a child of the sixties, I have grown up through the animated history of the women's movement, with its vigorous critique of the Established Church; and as an Anglican I have lived through the reluctant progress of the institution towards the ordination of women. This dualistic experience has resulted in a resigned attitude to marginalization; I tend to accept as inevitable that Christians and non-Christians alike will reject my political and theological views. The internalization of worthlessness that has stemmed from my experience of abuse, of womanhood, of being a single-parent in a mixed-heritage family, means it has taken me a long time to have confidence that it could be they, not me, who have got some of it wrong.

Whilst I have learnt much from research and academic study, I believe it is not the only or necessarily the best context in which to seek the truth. My theological understanding has been honed by a set of experiences that lead me to question some received wisdoms and sit uneasily with others. This is in essence a sincere attempt to deal with the otherwise insoluble difficulty that some of our experiences just don't connect with traditional hermeneutical thought, and some traditional doctrines just don't make sense in the light of our experience. It is more a creative and organic theological engagement[1] than a coherent dissertation. Like all theological thought, it is at best a work in progress.

My journey began with a critique of the mainstream theological doctrine and interpretation that can seem to favour abusive acts as justified in some circumstances (e.g. Lot's daughters), or as requested by God (e.g. the sacrifice of Isaac) or even as an appeasement to God's essential nature (e.g. a Christology of submission). I do not believe in an abusive God who is on the side of the oppressor. How, then, could I locate a theology that does not reinforce power abuse in home, church and social institutions?

I was surprised by fresh discoveries of theological perspectives inspired by survivors – the replacing of sin with joy and righteousness, a theology of powerlessness and the vision of a justice-based community of shalom. I returned to three images that speak powerfully into the survivor's journey – the experience of being the sacrificial lamb; the reclaiming of the child princess during the healing process; the desire for a rescuing angel and the ultimate experience of salvation offered and taken. I began to attempt to weave the voice of survivors into a releasing theology that removes the compulsion to forgive, condemns the collusion with violent abuse in all contexts and asks if Jesus' crucifixion is God doing self-harm? In some trepidation, I offer the resulting cloth of patches representing insights that have touched me, simply tacked together, working towards a survivor's theology, as a child of liberation theology similar to early womanist, black and feminist discoveries.

Sacrificial lambs

The place of the cross and Christ's suffering as central to the Christian faith cannot be disputed. The significance of the image and the act, as expressed in a variety of doctrines through the ages, remains a matter of dispute. Feminist and womanist theologies provide some of the main critiques that are echoed by a survivor's understanding.

Like the criticism of the traditional interpretation of Isaac's sacrifice,[2] atonement that is founded on a God who needs appeasing through ritual sacrifice presents obvious difficulties to a survivor. How can I believe in a loving father who saves me, if he would willingly give me up to my abusers? If as father he demands Jesus' sacrifice and there is no other possible way for salvation to be achieved, then he is no better than the man who abused me. The notion that Jesus is the ransom price to pay for our sins, *demanded* by God, provides a similar justification for the abuse of children and their silence 'to protect the family'. It is an echo of the blood sacrifice mindset of the ancient world.

The image held in tension to this is one of God as victim: not demanding a bloodletting but crucified by our continued choice of sin. In this image we are the torturers and abusers, and the death of Christ is the consequence of our actions, willingly embraced by Christ. Feminist theologians still have some problems with this. The idea of self-sacrifice has been used to oppress women in both secular and faith communities to this day. The emphasis on the silent acceptance of suffering and willing debasement has long been used to keep the oppressed in their place, from global to domestic slavery. This idea lingers behind the reluctance to report and intervene in domestic violence and the acceptance of those strands of Christianity which deny women roles of headship within the Church. It has the tainted smell of the glorification of suffering that expected black slaves in America and South Africa to remain content with their lot, for their rewards would be great in heaven. Like contemporary womanist theologians, I am as concerned with the here-and-now kingdom as with the anticipated one.

Before we sacrifice another gawky, 'spotless' lamb, we need to recognize the attractive magnetism between the practice and conceal-ment of abuse and the theological ideas that perpetuate it; responding to the 'imperative to a fundamental re-visioning of theology and all its component parts so that it ceases its complicity with the forces of oppression and abuse' (Pattinson, 1998, p. 39).

Digging Eden's dirt

Who was the abuser in this situation? Eve or the serpent? At one level this seems to speak of the obvious abuse by someone who leads another innocent astray and of how she then becomes pathologically blamed for leading the other. But at the very least Adam had equal responsibility for his decision as she had for hers. This illustrates the manipulation of an abuser (wily serpent, blaming the victim) and from the very beginning of human history, the ripple effect of abuse throughout generations. But is there a darker tale here? When I read this as a survivor, with the image I have been taught of a God that is omnipotent and omniscient, I have painful and frightening thoughts. As Eve, I see another picture of a manipulative leader, who entices me with forbidden fruit, knowing (because he created me) that I am curious and easily led, so as likely to make a bad choice as a good one. I see a God who – in a way – has groomed me to make the choice that will lead to my banishment from the garden – my punishment for a natural act in a circumstance he set up. I see an abuser who blames the victim rather than taking responsi-bility for his part in this situation.

It feels like a set-up and one that as a parent I would never dream of pushing my children into. Why didn't God create us with the capacity to make better moral choices? Why didn't he intervene to stop the serpent? Is inquisitiveness a result of sin or the natural character of a creative being? Didn't God know that saying 'don't do that' to adolescent humans is precisely the best way to get the opposite effect? As a colleague once suggested to me, here clearer than anywhere in the Bible is a story of adolescent angst, of growing up and leaving home. Compared to the transition I am trying to facilitate with my 'just left for university' son, this is not a happy example. This is not the God of unconditional love that I know and adore.

So what *is* the message here? I imagine it as the beginnings of a story of adolescence that reaches its conclusion in the tale of the prodigal son. Eden is the cocooned, protected world of childhood, a place of playfulness and abundance – what loving parent does not nurture and feed her children with generosity and joy? It is a safe space to practise and experiment and just to be, without responsibility or task. But humans were created in the image of God, with both male and female personae, with the capacity to learn, grow and fashion new life. The rhythm of organic life – life and death, decay and rebirth – is within our very nature and is the breathing – the spirit, if you like – of the earth. You have to dig in the dirt to garden. Gradually, safety becomes a limitation and our freedom to choose – whether or not our choices are wise – impels us towards leaving home. Our calling to parent the earth as God's companions ordains that we have that freedom, as do the emerging tribes of our children: 'Your children are not your children. They are the sons and daughters of Life's longing for itself. They come through you but not from you, and though they are with you yet they belong not to you' (Gibran, 1926, p. 26).

In this story, it is the serpent that represents the abuser. Establishing the pattern we have seen repeated many times, he grooms and tricks Eve into a choice that exploits her natural instincts (to trust, to be curious, to grow in wisdom). Adam – who may even have been there all the time (Genesis 3.6) – then makes the worst choice of his life. Human immaturity and frailty start the tolling of the bell of sin, which reverberates through each successive generation. As Romans 5.12–21 explains, one man's choice brings death, and this isn't resolved until one man's death brings life. On such small moments the world shudders and turns.

God appears to be angry with Eve and Adam for these childish mistakes, but I hear it not as anger towards them, but the anger born out of the agony of wisdom, knowing the dreadful implications for them, their descendants, the whole of life from this moment on. Too soon, mother God has lost her innocent children, too soon they have to deal with the consequences of abuse, she cannot make life go backwards, which she must have known from the start of that fated game of hide-and-seek. There is that angry relief all parents know in the first question: 'Who told you that you were naked?'; followed by the anguish and sorrow behind the second question, as the awful truth emerges: 'What is this you have done?'

At-one-ment

So the prodigal son has to live with the consequences of his actions and the parent has to grieve in separation, longing to wrap the children close to her again. Meanwhile the ripples of abuse keep spreading. In love, grief and anger, we reach the foot of the cross, this puzzle of the act of death that brings life. I agree with James Cone (1982, p. 17):

> Christian theology is a theology of liberation. It is a rational study of the being of God in the world in the light of the existential situation of an oppressed community, relating the forces of liberation to the essence of the gospel, which is Jesus Christ.

Like others who have criticized his early work, I believe he overlooked the centrality of reconciliation to the Christian message. Both liberation and reconciliation are equal partners in the model of restorative justice central to a survivors' theology.

This restoration of harmony is described once (Romans 5.11) in the King James Bible as atonement, an English word that described the reunion (at-one-ment) of two divided companies. Scholars inform us that the word is used here to translate the Greek *katallage*, literally meaning 'downing the otherness' and normally translated as reconciliation. In the old belief, atonement involved the repeated rites of repentance and sacrifice, to restore the covenant that the people persistently broke. In Jesus' parable of the prodigal son, this distorted image of a judgemental and punitive parent is replaced with a nurturing one who yearns only to embrace the lost child again. No additional sacrifice or repentance is demanded before the unreserved caress and kiss wrap the child to the parent's chest once more, like a breast-feeding mother. This 'homecoming' (Nouwen, 1994) enacts unconditional love in its most tender and joyful compassion.[3] The otherness of autonomy dissolves into a reconciliation that restores the birth-cord, and parent and child are again at one.

Suffering and the self-harm of the crucifixion

However, before the hug of family can be enjoyed, there comes the costly embrace of the passion. The significance of the crucifixion resonates with a survivor's experience of suffering and, for some, the torture of abuse: here is God inhabiting our experience and viewing the world from the depths of our pain. As Bonhoeffer understood (1971, p. 17), this perspective brings insight:

> We have for once learnt to see the great events of world history from below, from the perspective of the outcast, the suspects, the maltreated,

the powerless, the oppressed, the reviled – in short, from the perspective of those who suffer. The important thing is that neither bitterness nor envy should have gnawed at the heart during this time, that we should have come to look with new eyes at matters great and small, sorrow and joy, strength and weakness, that our perception of generosity, humanity, justice and mercy should have become clearer, freer, less corruptible.

God suffers with us; in doing so, does he also become our rescuer? I am as uneasy with rescuing angels as I am with sacrificial lambs, much as I have often prayed for God to send me an angel (armed with a loo-brush, to clear out all the rubbish!). In transactional analysis, the Rescuer is one role in the game of the drama triangle, played with the Persecutor and the Victim. There may be a Bystander, passively observing. A liberation that doesn't include my participation, confirms me in passive victim mode. Jesus on the cross as either victim or rescuer can imply a disempowering dynamic that also risks placing God in the role of persecutor. The triangle of the Trinity becomes a hierarchy, rather than Creator, Reconciler and Empowerer encircled in equal relationship.

Napper and Newton (2000, pp. 9.8–10, 9.21) explain the positive equivalents in the winner's triangle:

- The Victim becomes the Voice – expressing feelings and vulnerability.
- The Persecutor becomes Proactive – defining boundaries and powerfully loving and affirming.
- The Rescuer becomes Responsible – concerned for and responsive to others and doing what is required, no more and no less.
- The Bystander moves to Be Involved – perhaps a model is accompanist?

I see the cross as the platform for the Voice. Here is the drama of all abuse and oppression given expression beyond words – it is perhaps depicted most powerfully in art in the Brazilian image of the Tortured Christ. Here is an act of protest and witness that became the most powerful intervention, in the midst of weakness and vulnerability. Ironically, it is the insight provided by self-harm that has shaped this passion narrative. Self-harmers injure themselves in order to gain control over a situation of chaos and disorder that others have imposed on them. They may cut in an act of purification or to release their straining, pent-up emotions – anger, pain, and grief. It is the silenced struggling to give voice; because no one sees, hears or understands the abuse, self-injury makes inward emotional pain outward and visible. Why did Jesus have to be crucified publicly? If it was purely to pay a price for our sins, why didn't God choose a nice quiet murder in the back streets? Was the very method of crucifixion – like self-harm – a desperate attempt to communicate? The layers of meaning bring powerful echoes. On the cross the groanings of God from the heart and depths of creation (the body) are made manifest on the surface (the skin?) with the 'bright red scream' of real wounds. Embracing our pain and suffering is indeed a way to life, but is not the end of the journey. The cross is the signpost to the 'living beyond' of the resurrection of the body.

Body theology

Concetta Perot provides three biblical images of the body, which bring theological insight to our understanding of the strong link between all types of abuse, and all types of self-harm.[4] My experience in survivors' networks is that self-injury, alcohol and drug misuse and eating disorders are common issues that we struggle with. Exploration of these issues offers an alternative body image that is rooted in the warm and scarred flesh of the resurrected Christ.

Flesh

The foundation of Christian body theology is its integrity as God's creation. It can be defiled but can also be redeemed. Paul can be misunderstood here; when he talks about flesh, he does not refer to the body as opposed to the soul, rather an inclination towards sin or God. Christian asceticism in the Middle Ages saw the ultimate expression of this idea in the mortification of the flesh. The worldly orientation of both body and soul is denied through renunciation of all creature comforts; and the sufferings of Christ are embraced, in order to achieve greater union with God. This has been criticized as based on a dualistic view of human flesh, but I understand the mystics to have a holistic concept of our nature. It is a spiritual enlightenment and experience that is realized:

> I knew in my spirit that I had received the stigmata of your adorable and venerable wounds interiorly in my heart, just as though they had been made on the natural places of the body. By these wounds you not only healed my soul, but you gave me to drink of the inebriating cup of love's nectar.[5]

For an abuse survivor, there may indeed be a more dualistic understanding. The body may have become something hateful that has betrayed (through its responses) or been defiled (beyond redemption). Mortification or self-harm is an attempt to punish, purge, control. Or there may be strong echoes of the mystic approach. I may have so suppressed feelings of pain (in order to survive) that I need to hurt myself in order to feel; in order to feel love I must feel pain. The pain of the harming becomes a tool not to separate my flesh from the soul, but to integrate dissociative pieces of myself.

The affirmation of our goodness in creation emphasized by the incarnation and redeemed by Christ in resurrection can be a powerful and healing message for self-harmers. Identification with the Christ who has shared and understood our sufferings is the common experience of the oppressed, and confirms our place in the passion story.

Temple

This has been connected to the body image in several ways. First, the notion of the body as a temple within which God resides, an idea that leads to the view we should protect and respect our bodies or we are dishonouring God (1 Corinthians 6.18–20). There can be a strong flavour of that image in much self-harm; it can be an angry act, born from powerlessness and frustration, hurting what is safe and good precisely because one is powerless to direct the hurt where it really belongs. This is why it is a fallacy to perceive those who self-injure as a danger to others; it is more often a selfless act recreating one's victim status in order to protect the innocent and, ironically, the guilty. Jesus appeared to have a far more pragmatic approach, happy to eat and drink with sinners: 'Nothing outside you can make you "unclean" by going into you. Rather, it is what comes out of you that makes you "unclean"' (Mark 7.15–16). He was not unaware of the irony of prevailing attitudes:

> For John came neither eating nor drinking, and they say, 'He has a demon.' The Son of Man came eating and drinking and they say, 'Here is a glutton and a drunkard, a friend of tax collectors and "sinners".' But wisdom is proved right by her actions. (Matthew 11.18–20)

The second picture expresses our union with God:

> The Lord said to her: 'Behold my heart; now it will be your temple. And now look among the other parts of my body and choose for yourself other places in which you can lead a monastic life, because from now on my body will be your cloister.[6]

This is an invitation that speaks of love and grace. Instead of being condemned for punishing myself, I am offered another dwelling-place, where I can encounter God, offer myself and be ministered to.

Tent

Peter described the body as a tent – a temporary, moveable dwelling-place to be discarded when no longer needed (2 Peter 1.14). This apparent indifference may be a consequence of abuse and an attitude that condones neglect of our bodies, at the very least. Contemporary scientific understanding has both confirmed this separation of body and soul; and acted in counter-point to the idea that the body as matter is insignificant. This may underlie our ambivalent attitude. The body is both the problem and the channel for transformation. It is both to be denied and to be nourished.

Self-harmers usually find denial easier than appropriate care. Bulimia or binge eating may appear as overactive nourishment, but in fact are a form of further self-abuse. Learning to see myself as someone of worth, who deserves tender nurturing, will not happen simply by taking away the weapons I am using to injure myself. Indeed, this can be an extremely dangerous thing to do; self-harming is a generally successful coping strategy, usually a quite logical and responsible response to an extreme set of circumstances, and taking away one coping strategy before it has been replaced with another can leave me dangerously unprotected.

Reclaiming the image of the body as tent, neither insignificant nor unreachable, but with the simplicity of the tipi and the provision of the yurt, provides a positive solution. Gradually I can learn other ways to communicate my pain and anguish, to see truer reflections of myself, kinder treatments for my wounds. Meanwhile I don't need to get too hung up about it; it is simply the honest tent of a travelling pilgrim, which I can bring with me on my long journey. I can also understand it as my 'safe space' or sanctuary, where my abuser can no longer reach me. And the God who squats on the rug of my tent with me is far more reassuring and approachable than the ruler in his palace.

The tent of sanctuary

The narrative of the People of God's escape to safety provides a source of hope for all Christians facing adversity. It is the covenant promise and the crucifixion fulfilment. I noted in Chapter 2 how this could lead to a difficult place for Christian survivors, because whether the abuse continued for many years, or was a single occasion, there was during its occurrence, no real escape.

> As a child, I used to dream of dramatic rescue. I invented stories in my head – sometimes while the abuse was taking place – of Aslan leaping through the wall, pushing my Dad to the ground, me climbing on his back and we fly out through the window. When that didn't happen, the stories evolved into me, a tomboy little heroine, rescuing lots of other people from desperate situations. When the abuse still didn't stop, I gave up creating stories . . .[7]

For some Christian survivors, God seems to have moved here from being involved to becoming a disinterested or powerless bystander. Many of us have raged Job-like at a God who moved the infant Jesus out into the comparative safety of Egypt but abandoned us to the fate of the slaughtered innocents. The witness of the resurrection is that there was sanctuary, even in the experience of the abuse. The most powerful description of this I have ever read is in Bishop Desmond Tutu's book about the South African Truth and Reconciliation Commission. He relates the story of a woman who was tortured and raped in detention and found a desperate way to survive. As she described it, she took her soul out of her body and put it in the corner of the cell, so with the eyes of her spirit she could watch her body's mistreatment as though it was happening to someone else. The tale ends (p. 107): 'She said with tears in her eyes that she had not yet gone back to that room to fetch her soul and that it was still sitting in the corner where she had left it.'

This story caught me with a profound resonance. Perhaps God's intervention was to keep my soul safe, in a situation where man's inhumanity to (wo)man was not preventable without God becoming persecutor or rescuer. So God neither colluded nor abandoned, but provided sanctuary even within the very context of the abuse itself. Perhaps the journey to healing is my own part in returning to fetch my soul, gather her up and tend her scars. Or maybe it is my soul that has to make the journey to be restored to the wounded body. The resurrection is the hope and promise and reality of that reunion.

DISCUSSION QUESTIONS

To discuss
What is your understanding of the drama in the Garden of Eden? Do you see an abuser, a victim, and any other roles? How do you interpret God's anger at the end of the story? What does this mean for your understanding of sin and abuse?

To reflect
Reflect on the image of the prodigal son being embraced by the loving father. If you can get a print or postcard of the Rembrandt painting that inspired Henri Nouwen, even better. When have you experienced this homecoming? What might it mean to a survivor or a perpetrator of abuse?

To do
The roles suggested in the winner's triangle – voice, proactive, responsible, involved – provide a pattern for positive relationships. Can you identify a pattern in your own behaviour or relationships where a change in role would be positive? Does this model bring any insights to your understanding of the Trinity?

Notes

1 Thanks to Professor John Hull for this term, on a Christian adult education discussion forum, some years ago.
2 We are familiar with this as a story of Abraham put to the test by God. Isaac is the sacrifice, because it gives value to Abraham's fidelity and because, culturally, the child then had no individual rights but was an expression of the corporate family community. Some have suggested a different meaning. At the time, the Molochites routinely practised child sacrifice as part of their religious ritual. In this context God's message could be seen not as one of seeking unquestioning obedience but rather of challenging this inhumane practice – Yahweh does not desire a child to be killed.
3 Nouwen's book, inspired by the Rembrandt painting *The Return of the Prodigal Son*, explores the homecoming of both younger and elder son into the embrace of the father, from the well-known parable.
4 Concetta Perot, Greenbelt seminar, 2003, 'I punish my body', unpublished.
5 Gertrude the Great of Helfta, 1256–1302, quoted in Obbard, 2002, p. 25.
6 Gertrude the Great in Obbard, 2002, p. 39.
7 Quote from survivor, used with permission.

References

Bonhoeffer, D., *Letters and Papers from Prison* (enlarged edn), SCM Press, London, 1971.
Cone, J., *A Black Theology of Liberation*, New York, Orbis Books, 1982.
Gibran, K., *The Prophet*, Heinemann, London, 1926 (1980 edn).
Hunt, M., *Fierce Tenderness: A Feminist Theology of Friendship*, Crossroad, New York, 1992.
Napper, R. and Newton, T., *Tactics: transactional analysis concepts for all trainers, teachers and tutors, plus insight into collaborative learning strategies*, TA Resources, Ipswich, 2000.
Nouwen, H. J. M., *The Return of the Prodigal Son: A Story of Homecoming*, Darton, Longman & Todd, London, 1994.
Obbard, E. R., *Medieval Women Mystics*, New City Press, New York, 2002.
Pattinson, S., 'Suffer Little Children: The Challenge of Child Abuse and Neglect to Theology', *Theology and Sexuality, Journal of the Centre for the Study of Christianity and Sexuality*, No. 9, September 1998.
Tutu, D., *No Future Without Forgiveness*, Rider, London, 1999.

10

A Piece of Bread:
resources and sources of help

———◀◦▶———

This chapter signposts a range of resources to support different areas of the practice considered. The title comes from a story about child holocaust victims; once 'rescued' they couldn't sleep without the security and comfort of a piece of bread that kept alive the hope they would still eat tomorrow. Not only is this a powerful metaphor for survivors, it also describes the role of books and resources to give us confidence when we venture into new areas and to support and symbolize our development and progress.

How to find what you need

The resources are grouped together in sections under broad headings, starting with general resources for all types of abuse, followed by additional specialist organizations. Generally I have placed organizations and publications in what I judge to be the most appropriate category, in order to provide a reasonable range of initial contacts and ideas. Some key resources are listed in more than one section. Inevitably there are some gaps and the list is not exhaustive (it would be too long!). I have aimed to provide a good starting point; any of these contacts will lead to other suggestions you may also wish to pursue. Each section includes organizations and published resources. Many organizations provide a wide range of services, such as training, that have grown out of their key focus, such as survivor support. So it is worth looking in several sections to find what you need. There are many more resources in the area of child protection than adult abuse; although child-focused, some of these have useful information and practice ideas that can be adapted for supporting survivors and dealing with incidents of adult abuse too. The main headings are:

1 Helplines (p. 156) – for reporting, crisis work and information and advice;
2 Survivors Support (p. 156) – healing support, advocacy and resources for survivors;
3 Training, consultancy and policy development (p. 161);
4 Worship and theology resources (p. 163);
5 Families, children and young people – including domestic violence (p. 164);
6 Spiritual, pastoral and power abuse (p. 171);
7 Abusers and those at risk of abusing (p. 173) – support and working with them.

1 Helplines

The following helplines can be contacted if you have any concerns about abuse, whether you are a child or an adult, whether you are being abused or are a survivor, have concerns about someone else or are a leader dealing with a situation of abuse. They offer a range of support, advice and information services. The particular focus of each service is indicated.

In emergencies contact the police or your local Social Services 24-hour number.

NSPCC	0808 800 5000	*– for anyone concerned that a child is at risk*
CCPAS	0845 120 4551	*– any child abuse issues, a Christian agency*
Childline	0800 1111	*– support for any child needing to talk*
Women's Aid	0808 2000 247	*– support for families experiencing domestic violence*
Samaritans	08457 90 90 90	*– support for anyone in distress*
POPAN	0845 450 0300	*– help for cases of professional abuse*
Family Matters	01474 537392	*– for survivors and non-abusing family members*
Young Minds	0800 018 2138	*– for anyone concerned about a child's mental health*
NAPAC	0800 085 3330	*– support for adults abused as children*
Parentline Plus	0808 800 2222	*– support for parents with any concerns*
Saneline	0845 767 8000	*– for anyone in mental distress and their supporters*
RESPOND	0808 808 0700	*– for survivors or abusers with learning difficulties*

2 Survivors' support

These are agencies and websites offering support to survivors of all types of abuse. Also included are some agencies working in the mental health field that may be particularly useful for survivors and their supporters. Many of these resources will also be helpful for family and friends of survivors and professionals working within the abuse field.

S:VOX – A voice for abuse survivors and those who support them
c/o St James' Church, 236 Mitcham Lane, London SW16 6NT.
Email: <info@svox.org.uk> Web: <http://www.svox.org.uk>
A new organization set up by survivors for survivors of any sort of abuse, as a child or as an adult, including emotional, physical, sexual and spiritual abuse. Offering support, education and advocacy including a new fledgling network of self-help groups.

Christian Survivors of Sexual Abuse (CSSA)
c/o 38 Sydenham Villas Rd, Cheltenham, Glos. GL52 6DZ.
CSSA offers self-help support to survivors of childhood sexual abuse. There are self-help groups, a newsletter and occasional retreats and services of worship. Help is offered to churches and groups wanting to plan their own survivor-orientated service. They also publish prayer cards and a helpful booklet for churches.

Minister and Clergy Sexual Abuse Survivors (MACSAS)
PO Box 46933, London E8 1XA.
Support and networking for people who have experienced sexual abuse by clergy or others in ministry.

National Association for People Abused in Childhood (NAPAC)
42 Curtain Road, London EC2A 3NH.
Freephone 0800 085 3330 Monday–Friday: 12 noon–8 p.m., Saturday: 9 a.m.–12 noon.
Email: <Email@napac.fsnet.co.uk> Web: <http://www.napac.org.uk>
Support, campaigning, information, literature for survivors and their supporters and an information line supporting adults who were abused in childhood.

The Samaritans
The Upper Mill, Kingston Road, Ewell, Surrey KT17 2AF.
Tel: 08457 90 90 90
Web: <http://www.samaritans.org.uk>
Helpline and on-line support for anyone in despair.

Association of Christian Counsellors
29 Momus Boulevard, Coventry CV2 5NA.
Tel: 0845 124 9569, 0845 124 9570
Email: <mail@acc-uk.org> Web: <http://www.acc-uk.org>
National agency to promote best practice in Christian counselling and pastoral care. Provides referral service.

The British Association for Counselling and Psychotherapy (BACP)
BACP House, 35–7 Albert Street, Rugby, War. CV21 2SG.
Tel: 0870 443 5252
Web: <http://www.bacp.co.uk>
Professional body for therapists, provides lists of qualified therapists and guidance on good practice.

The Prevention of Professional Abuse Network (POPAN)
52–53 Russell Square, London WC1B 4HP.
Helpline: 0845 450 0300
Email: <info@popan.org.uk> Web: <http://www.popan.org.uk>
In addition to support for people who have experienced professional abuse, POPAN provides training and consultancy to voluntary and statutory organizations on abuse prevention and response.

Women's Aid Federation (England)
PO Box 391, Bristol BS99 7WS.
Tel: 0117 944 4411 Helpline: 0808 2000 247
Web: <http://www.womensaid.org.uk>
Women's Aid Helpline, Northern Ireland Tel: 028 9033 1818
Welsh Women's Aid Tel: 029 2039 0874
Scottish Women's Aid National Office Tel: 0131 475 2372
Support, advice, information and referrals for women experiencing domestic violence. Makes direct referrals to refuges. Also training, research and policy development.

Refuge National Crisis Line
Tel: 0870 599 5443
Offers support, information, referrals. Runs own refuges in London and South East.

Kiran – Asian Women's Aid
Tel: 020 8558 1986
Advice, support, refuge for Asian women, and women from other cultures, e.g. Turkey, Iran, Morocco, Malaysia etc.

MIND
Granta House, 15–19 Broadway, Stratford, London E15 4BQ.
Helpline/Mindinfoline: 0845 766 0163
Web: <http://www.mind.org.uk>
Contact for details of your local MIND association, support and training for people experiencing mental distress and mental health services users and staff.

Young Minds
102–108 Clerkenwell Rd, London EC1M 5SA.
Tel: 020 7336 8445 Information service: 0800 018 2138
Web: <http://www.youngminds.org.uk>
Campaigning, training and resources for mental health services for young people and children. Helpline provides information and advice for anyone concerned about a young person's mental health.

The Ann Craft Trust (ACT)
The ACT Centre for Social Work, University of Nottingham, University Park, Nottingham NG7 2RD. Tel: 0115 951 5400
Email: <information@anncrafttrust.org>
Web: <http://www.anncrafttrust.org>

Information, training, peer support and education aimed at protecting
adults and children with learning disabilities from abuse.

RESPOND
Third Floor, 24–32 Stephenson Way, London NW1 2HP.
Tel: 020 7383 0700 Helpline: 0808 808 0700
Email: <services@respond.org.uk> Web: <http://www.respond.org.uk>
Support and information for people with learning difficulties who have
been sexually abused including those who have perpetrated abuse. Also
training for those working with them.

Survivors on the Net
Web: <http://www.survivors.org.uk>
Support, resources, good practice, campaigning and networking for
survivors and supporters.

Help for Adult Victims of Child Abuse (HAVOCA)
Ty Newydd, London Road, Gwalchmai, Anglesey, N. Wales LL65 4PR.
Email: (general enquiries) <info@havoca.org>
(advice/support) <friend@havoca.org>
Provide support, information and education to adult victims of child abuse.
The site also has forums and bulletin boards.

Survivors Network of those Abused by Priests (SNAP)
Web: <http://www.survivorsnetwork.org>
International website for those abused by clergy.

<http://www.stardrift.net/survivor/>
Comprehensive site by UK survivor.

One in Four
219 Bromley Rd, Bellingham, London SE6 2PG.
Tel: 020 8697 2112
Email: <admin@oneinfour.org.uk> Web: <http://www.oneinfour.org.uk>
Counselling, support and training for survivors of sexual abuse and those
who support them.

Fire in Ice
89 Rodney Street, Liverpool L1 9AR.
Helpline: 0151 707 2614 (Monday only 5 p.m.–9 p.m.) Office Tel: 0151
708 6339 (Monday–Friday 10 a.m.–6 p.m.)
Web: <http://www.fireinice.co.uk>
Self-help project run by and for adult men who have experienced
childhood abuse, especially while in care institutions.

Relate
Tel: 01788 573241
Web: <http://www.relate.org.uk>
Counselling for people with relationship difficulties, whether married or
not.

CROP
Suite 21, Munro House, Duke Street, Leeds LS9 8AG.
Tel: 0113 2436896
Email: <crop1@freeuk.com>
A charity set up to end the sexual exploitation of children and young people by pimps and traffickers. Campaigning, support for parents and for young people working as prostitutes, publications and training for agencies.

Self Harm Alliance (SHA)
PO Box 61, Cheltenham, Glos. GL51 8YB.
Helpline: 01242 578820
Email: <support@selfharmalliance.org>
Web: <http://www.selfharmalliance.org>
Survivor-led voluntary group supporting people who self-harm.

National Self Harm Network (NSHN)
PO Box 7264, Nottingham NG1 6WJ.
Email: <info@nshn.co.uk> Web: <http://www.nshn.co.uk>
Support, information and training for people who self-harm and their supporters.

Anorexia Bulimia Care (ABC)
PO Box 173, Letchworth, Herts. SG6 1XQ.
Tel: 01462 423 351
Email: <anorexiabulimiacare@ntlworld.com>
Web: <http://www.anorexiabulimiacare.co.uk>
Christian organization providing support, resources and information for people who self-harm and their supporters.

Kidscape
2 Grosvenor Gardens, London SW1W 0DH.
Tel: 020 7730 3300 or 08451 205204 (local rate) (Mondays to Fridays 10 a.m.–4p.m.)
Website: <http://www.kidscape.org.uk>
Charity committed to keeping children safe from harm or any kind of abuse, including bullying. Provides telephone advice to anyone with concerns about school bullying. Publications for parents and children on child safety and the prevention of bullying.

Other good websites for children and young people:
<http://www.bullying.co.uk>
<http://www.childline.org.uk>

Published resources
Most published resources deal with specific abuse contexts, such as child sexual abuse, and are listed under the relevant sections for that context.

The Survivors' Directory
An essential resource for anyone supporting survivors of abuse.
<http://www.survivorsdirectory.org>

Directory and Books Services (DABS)
1 Broxholme Lane, Doncaster DN1 2LJ.
Tel: 01302 768 689
Email: <order@dabsbooks.co.uk> Web: <http://www.dabsbooks.co.uk>
Books and information for people who have been abused, supporters
and professionals. Publish an information pack for survivors and the
comprehensive National Resource Directory, which includes resources
and organizations, information and helpsheets on abuse, sexual assault,
domestic violence, recovery and prevention. Updated regularly.

Bass, Ellen and Davis, Laura, *The Courage to Heal*, Vermilion, London,
1997.
A very helpful and comprehensive book for survivors and supporters.

Herman, Judith L., *Trauma and Recovery: From domestic Abuse to*
Political Terror, Basic Books, New York, 1997.
Excellent book on the dynamics of trauma and the healing process.

Miller, Alice, *The Truth Will Set You Free*, Basic Books, New York, 2003.
One of many books by this recommended author and practitioner,
connecting childhood abuse with trauma and describing how to release the
truth in order to heal.

Strong, Marilee, *A Bright Red Scream: self-mutilation and the language of*
pain, Virago, London, 2000.
One of the best books around about self-harm, its root causes and
possibilities for healing.

3 Training, consultancy and policy development

I have not been able to find many agencies offering general services
covering different types of abuse; they mainly specialize in one field, such
as child protection. A few more general resources are highlighted below.
For advice and assistance with policy and training regarding abuse and
good practice, you should contact:

Organizations
Your denominational or organizational headquarters (who may offer
policies and training).

Trauma and Abuse Group (TAG)
PO Box 465, Godalming, Surrey GU7 2YL.
Tel: 01793 528077
Email: <chairman@tag-uk.net> Web: <http://www.tag-uk.net>
A group studying and supporting work concerning trauma, abuse and
dissociation. Provides newsletter, training, networking, consultancy and
information. Welcomes contribution of survivors.

S:VOX – A voice for abuse survivors and those who support them
(See section 2, p. 157.)

The Prevention of Professional Abuse Network (POPAN)
(See section 2, p. 158.)

Church Pastoral Aid Society (CPAS)
Athena Drive, Tachbrook Park, Warwick CV34 6NG.
Tel: 01926 458458
Email: <info@cpas.org.uk> Web: <http://www.cpas.org.uk>
Support, training and resources for church leadership including work with children, young people and families.

The Claybury Trust
PO Box 108, Edgware HA8 0YR.
Tel: 020 8906 2737
Email: <info@Claybury.com> Web: <http://www.claybury.org>
Provides encouragement, healing and resources for Christian ministers and leaders, including training, consultancy, counselling and resources.

Association of Christian Counsellors
(See section 2, p. 156.)

The British Association for Counselling and Psychotherapy (BACP)
(See section 2, p. 156.)

WAVE Trust (Worldwide Alternatives to ViolencE)
Cameron House, 61 Friends Rd, Croydon CR0 1ED.
Tel: 020 8688 3773
Email: <wavetrust@aol.com> Web: <http://www.wave.org>
Global organization dedicated to understanding the causes of violence and promoting effective, practical solutions.

Advisory, Conciliation and Arbitration Service (ACAS)
Helpline: 08457 47 47 47
Web: <http://www.acas.org.uk>
ACAS is a good starting point for general independent advice, information and publications about good practice in the context of employment, including disciplinary and grievance procedures.

The National Council for Voluntary Organizations (NCVO)
Regent's Wharf, 8 All Saints Street, London N1 9RL.
Tel: 020 7713 6161 Fax: 020 7713 6300 Helpdesk: 0800 2 798 798
Email: <ncvo@ncvo-vol.org.uk> Web: <http://www.ncvo-vol.org.uk>
For general advice and publications concerning good practice in the voluntary sector, NCVO is a key national umbrella organization with a good information service.

The Information Commissioner's Office
Wycliffe House, Water Lane, Wilmslow, Cheshire SK9 5AF.
Tel: 01625 545745
Email: <mail@ico.gsi.gov.uk>
Web: <http://www.informationcommissioner.gov.uk>
For data protection advice and resources

Published resources
For government health and safety publications contact HSE Books, PO Box 1999, Sudbury, Suffolk CO10 2WA. Tel: 01787 881165
Web: <http://www.hsebooks.co.uk>

Adirondack, Sandy, *Just about Managing? Effective management for voluntary organizations and community groups*, London Voluntary Service Council, London, 1998.
Comprehensive and useable resources covering all areas of good practice in management for voluntary groups, including disciplinary and grievance procedures, vetting, training, etc.

See section 5 for sources of good practice guidance for the youth, children's and families sector.

4 Worship and theology

Published resources
Burgess, Ruth and Galloway, Kathy (eds), *Praying for the Dawn: A Resource Book for the Ministry of Healing*, Wild Goose Publications, Glasgow, 2000.
A creative and practical resource for insightful worship and healing ministry.

Galloway, Kathy (ed.), *The Pattern of Our Days: Liturgies and Resources for Worship*, Wild Goose Publications, Glasgow, 1996.
Wild Goose are one of the few groups creating worship resources that deal with abuse and domestic violence among other current justice issues. This collection includes a liturgy concerned with women who have been abused and one on places of safety for all ages.

Galloway, Kathy (ed.), *Dreaming of Eden: Reflections on Christianity and Sexuality*, Wild Goose Publications, Glasgow, 1997.
Theological reflections and personal insights on sexuality, including abuse.

McFadyen, Alistair, *Bound to Sin: Abuse, Holocaust and the Christian Doctrine of Sin*, Cambridge University Press, Cambridge, 2000.
Systematic and practical theology that engages with the concrete reality of abuse.

Poling, James, *The Abuse of Power: A Theological problem*, Abingdon Press, Nashville, TN, 1991.

Time for Action: Sexual abuse, the Churches and a new dawn for survivors. The Report to Churches Together in Britain and Ireland of the Group established to examine issues of Sexual Abuse, Churches Together in Britain and Ireland, London, 2002.
Includes good theology chapter and worship resources.

Yancey, Philip, *What's so Amazing About Grace?*, Zondervan Publishing House, Grand Rapids, MI, 1997.
A compelling look at grace and forgiveness – no 'quick fix', lots of inspiration.

Other good worship anthologies include:

Morley, Janet, *All Desires Known*, SPCK, London, 1992.

Ward, Hannah and Wild, Jennifer, *Human Rites: Worship Resources for an Age of Change*, Mowbray, London, 1995.

Ward, Hannah and Wild, Jennifer (eds), *Celebrating Women,* SPCK, London, 1995.

The Methodist Church publishes worship resources on special themes including an annual service for 'Women Against Violence' Sunday, which has focused on domestic violence. See their website <http://www.methodist.org.uk/prayer>

Two good alternative worship websites that have links to lots of resources:

<http://www.alternativeworship.org>
<http://www.sacramentis.com>

5 Children and families, including child protection, child abuse and domestic violence

Many organizations offer a range of services and resources for children, families and those working with them, including work on child abuse and child protection. I have listed training and good practice agencies separately, as there are so many organizations working in this field. I have not put domestic violence in a separate category, as many child and family agencies work across child protection and domestic violence fields, and many children experience both.

Organizations
National Society for the Prevention of Cruelty to Children (NSPCC)
42 Curtain Rd, London EC2A 3NH.
Tel: 020 7825 2500 Helpline: 0808 800 5000
Web: <http://www.nspcc.org.uk>
Information, training, research, campaigns and resources aimed at protecting children. Project teams working across the country in a range of child protection services including support, investigation and prevention.

Churches Child Protection Advisory Service (CCPAS)
PO Box 133, Swanley, Kent BR8 7UQ.
Helpline: 0845 120 4551 Fax: 0845 120 4552
Email: <info@ccpas.co.uk> Web: <http://www.ccpas.co.uk>
Information, training, resources for churches and Christian groups of any denomination aimed at child protection and related issues including fostering and adoption. Assistance with policy development and CRB checking service for registered groups. Helpline offers advice and support to leaders and others with individual cases as well as any child protection issue.

Women's Aid Federation
(See section 2, p. 158.)

Childwatch
19 Spring Bank, Hull HU3 1AF.
Tel: 01482 325 552 (Mondays to Fridays 9 a.m.–5 p.m.)
E-mail: <info@childwatch.org.uk> Web: <http://www.childwatch.org.uk>

Aims to assist community prevention of family violence and child abuse, by raising public and professional awareness. Provides confidential advice and counselling to victims of physical, mental and sexual abuse. Produces information packs.

Kidscape
(See section 2, p. 160.)

NEWPIN
National Newpin, Sutherland House, 35 Sutherland Square, Walworth, London SE17 3EE.
Tel: 020 7358 5900
Email: <info@newpin.org.uk> Web: <http://www.newpin.org.uk>
Helps parents under stress break the cycle of destructive family behaviour. Has network of local centres offering a range of services for parents and children.

Voice for the Child in Care
Unit 4 Pride Court, 80–82 White Lion Street, London N1 9PF.
Tel: 020 7833 5792
Email: <info@vcc-uk.org> Web: <http://www.vcc-uk.org>
Provides free advocacy and support for children and young people who are in contact with Social Services and having problems with them.

Save the Children
1 St John's Lane, London EC1M 4AR.
Tel: 020 7012 6400
Email: <supporter.care@savethechildren.org.uk>
Web: <http://www.savethechildren.org.uk>
Working internationally in prevention and response to children at risk, including projects and resources.

The Lucy Faithfull Foundation
Bordesley Hall, The Holloway, Alvechurch, Birmingham B48 7QA.
Tel: 01527 591922
Email: <referrals@lucyfaithfull.org> or <training@lucyfaithfull.org>
Provides assessment and intervention programmes for adults and young people who sexually abuse; also support for non-abusing family members and survivors. They run a training programme for people working in the child protection and child abuse field, based on their particular expertise, including training for faith-based organizations.

Parentline Plus
520 Highgate Studios, 53–79 Highgate Road, Kentish Town, London NW5 1TL.
Helpline: 0808 800 2222 (24 hours) Free textphone: 0800 783 6783 (Mondays to Fridays 9 a.m.–5 p.m.)
Web: <http://www.parentlineplus.org.uk>
Offers support on all aspects of parenting to anyone involved in caring for children. The helpline is free and confidential and offers support, listening and information on all issues of concern.

Barnardo's
Tanners Lane, Barkingside, Ilford, Essex IG6 1QG.
Tel: 020 8550 8822
Email: <dorothy.howes@barnardos.org.uk>
Web: <http://www.barnardos.org.uk>
Campaigning, research and projects for families, children and young people.

The Children's Society
Edward Rudolf House, Margery Street, London WC1X 0JL.
Tel: 0845 300 1128
Email: <supporteraction@childrenssociety.org.uk>
Web: <http://www.the-childrens-society.org.uk>
Campaigning, research and projects for families, children and young people.

<http://www.watton.org/abuse>
Comprehensive church-run website on child protection.

Children are Unbeatable Alliance
94 White Lion Street, London N1 9TS.
Tel: 020 7713 0569
Web: <http://www.childrenareunbeatable.org.uk>
An alliance of more than 300 agencies campaigning for children to have the same legal protection against being hit as adults. Also advice on disciplining children without smacking.

Mothers of Sexually Abused Children (MOSAC)
c/o West Greenwich Community & Arts Centre, 141 Greenwich High Road, London SE10 8JA.
Freephone 0800 980 1958
Web: <http://www.mosac.org.uk>
Telephone advice, information and support for mothers and female carers of children who have been sexually abused.

The British Association for the Study and Prevention of Child Abuse and Neglect (BASPCAN)
10 Priory St, York YO1 6EZ.
Tel: 01904 613605
Email: <baspcan@baspcan.org.uk> Web: <http://www.baspcan.org.uk>
Education, campaigning and publication aimed at preventing child abuse.

The Association of Child Abuse Lawyers (ACAL)
Tel: 01923 286 888
Web: <http://www.childabuselawyers.com>
Practical support for lawyers and other professionals working for adults and children who have been abused. ACAL can give survivors of abuse details of lawyers experienced in this area. ACAL can advise you on reporting child abuse which took place a number of years ago.

<http://www.abuselaw.co.uk>
Information and guidance on the legal process for child and adult survivors of abuse.

NCH
85 Highbury Park, London N5 1UD.
Tel: 0845 7 626 579 (Monday–Friday 9 a.m.–5 p.m.)
Web: <http://www.nch.org.uk>
Children's charity with useful information on keeping your children safe while they surf the internet.

The Internet Watch Foundation
Voicemail: 0845 600 8844
Email: <admin@iwf.org.uk> Web: <http://www.iwf.org.uk>
An independent organization which aims to address the problem of illegal material on the internet, in particular child abuse.

Child protection training
For advice and assistance with child protection policy and training, you should contact:

Your denominational or organizational headquarters' Child Protection Officer

Your Area Child Protection Committee (via local authority social services) – these may change their title or role when the provisions of the new Children's Bill are implemented.

CCPAS and NSPCC both provide training and consultancy services (contact details as above).

Good practice resources for youth and children's work
For advice, training and assistance in adopting good practice in working with children, young people and families you should contact:

Your denominational or organizational headquarters' Youth or Children's Officer.

Any of the major youth or children's work organizations.

Your local authority youth and children's services – the title varies across the country.

Some useful agencies include:

Centre for Youth Ministry
PO Box 442, Swindon SN5 7JH.
Tel: 01793 418336 Fax: 01793 418118
Email: <admin@centreforyouthministry.ac.uk>
Web: <http://www.centreforyouthministry.ac.uk>
Full and part-time training for volunteers and paid workers including initial training to degree level and in-service training to postgraduate level.

The National Youth Agency (NYA)
17–23 Albion Street, Leicester LE1 6GD.
Tel: 0116 285 3792
Email: <dutydesk@nya.org.uk> Web: <http://www.nya.org.uk>

Information and resources, including training courses for professional and vocational qualifications, for all who work with young people.

Oasis Trust
115 Southwark Bridge Road, London SE1 0AX.
Tel: 020 7450 9000
Email: <enquiries@oasistrust.org> Web: <http://www.oasistrust.org>
Christian organization active in youth and community action. Training courses for youth workers.

Youth for Christ (YFC)
Head Office, PO Box 5254, Halesowen, West Midlands B63 3DG.
Tel: 0121 550 8055 Fax: 0121 550 9979.
Email: <yfc@yfc.co.uk> Web: <http://www.yfc.co.uk>
Youth projects and training, resources and information for anyone working with young people.

Youthwork Magazine
CCP, PO Box 17911, London SW1P 4YX.
Tel: 020 7316 1450
Email: <youthwork@premier.org.uk> Web: <http://www.youthwork.co.uk>
Magazine, resources and training for Christian youth work.

UK Youth
2nd Floor, Kirby House, 20–24 Kirby Street, London EC1N 8TS.
Tel: 020 7242 4045
Email: <info@ukyouth.org> Web: <http://www.ukyouth.org>
Information, training and resources for all working with young people.

National Association of Clubs for Young People
371 Kennington Lane, London SE11 5QY.
Tel: 020 7793 0787
Email: <office@nacyp.org.uk> Web: <http://www.nacyp.org.uk>
Network of projects and support, information and training for those working with young people.

Children's Ministry
26 Lottbridge Drove, Eastbourne BN23 6NT.
Tel: 01323 437749
Email: <childrensministry@kingsway.co.uk>
Web: <http://www.childrensministry.co.uk>
Resources, conference and training for children's ministry.

Catholic Youth Ministry
National Office, 415 Michigan Avenue NE, Suite 40, Washington, DC, 20017, USA.
Tel: +1 2002 636 3825
Email: <info@nfcym.org> Web: <http://nfcym.org>

The Children's Legal Centre
University of Essex, Wivenhoe Park, Colchester, Essex CO4 3SQ.
Advice line: 01206 873820 (Monday to Friday 10 a.m.–12.30 p.m.)
Administration/Publications: 01206 872466

Email: <clc@essex.ac.uk> Web: <http://www.childrenslegalcentre.com>
Information, advice and publications regarding children and young people and the law, including children's rights and legal matters affecting good practice.

Sure Start
DfES, Level 2, Caxton House, Tothill St, London SW1H 9NA.
Tel: 0870 000 2288
Email: <info.surestart@dfes-gsi.gov.uk>
Web: <http://www.surestart.gov.uk>
Government programmes for childcare, early learning and family support.

Other Christian youth and children's work training providers include:

Moorlands College
Sopley, Christchurch, Dorset BI I23 7AT.
Tel: 01425 672369
Email: <mailto:mpi@moorlands.ac.uk>
Web: <http://www.moorlands.ac.uk>

Nazarene Theological College
Dene Road, Didsbury, Manchester M20 2GU.
Tel: 0161 445 3063
Email: <mailto:prae@nazarene.ac.uk> Web: <http://www.nazarene.ac.uk>

University College of Chester
Dept of Theology and Religious Studies, Parkgate Road, Chester CH1 4BJ.
Tel: 01244 375444
Email: <mailto:d.gosling@chester.ac.uk> Web: <http://www.chester.ac.uk>

Government and key agency good practice documents
Catholic Bishops' Conference of England and Wales, *Healing the Wounds, Catholic Bishops' Conference of England and Wales*, 1994. (*Considers child victims in the church.*)

Christian Survivors of Sexual Abuse (CSSA), *Safe Church: Safe Children*, BM-CSSA, 1997.

Church of Ireland, *Safeguarding Trust*, Church of Ireland Office, 1997 (2nd edn 2000).

Home Office, *Safe from Harm*, HMSO, London, 1993.

National Children's Bureau, *Taking Care: A Response to Children, Adults and Abuse for Churches and Other Faith Communities*, NCB, Leicester, 1992 (2nd edn 1997).

Nolan, Lord, *A Programme for Action: Final Report of the Independent Review in Child Sexual Protection in the Catholic Church in England and Wales*, Catholic Bishops' Conference of England and Wales, 2001. (*Covers dealing with offenders too.*)

Salvation Army, *Safe and Sound*, Salvation Army, 1996 (2nd edn 2000).

Working Together to Safeguard Children: A Guide to Interagency Working to Safeguard and Promote the Welfare of Children, HMSO, London, 1999.

Published resources
Ainscough, Carolyn and Toon, Kay, *Breaking Free, Help for survivors of child sexual abuse*, Sheldon Press, London, 1993.
A practical and helpful book for survivors – UK written, workbook available, good for young people and adults.

Cashman, Hilary, *Christianity and Child Sexual Abuse*, SPCK, London, 1993.
A helpful general exploration of abuse and the issues for Christians.

Cawson, Pat, Wattam, Corinne, Brooker, Sue and Kelly, Graham, *Child Maltreatment in the United Kingdom: A study of the prevalence of child abuse and Neglect*, NSPCC, 2000.

Conway, Helen, *Domestic Violence and the Church*, Paternoster Press, Cumbria, 1998.
An examination of the causes and effects of domestic violence, sources of support and an excellent range of interventions to its eradication.

Corby, Brian (ed.), *Child Abuse*, Open University Press, 2000.
The author explores child abuse and neglect from a historical viewpoint, and looks at the shift towards more preventive, family supportive approaches to child protection work.

Gibbs, Peter, *Child Sexual Abuse: A Concern for the Church?* Grove Books, Cambridge, 1992.
Accessible, knowledgeable and compassionate introduction to sexual abuse and the challenge to the church to respond with healing support for survivors and perpetrators.

Gosney, Jeanette, *Surviving Child Sexual Abuse*, Grove Books, Cambridge, 2002.
An accessible booklet that gives excellent insight into the experience of church and spirituality faced by survivors, helpful and unhelpful theologies and practical ways churches can respond more appropriately.

Hansen, Tracy, *Seven for a Secret . . . Healing the wounds of sexual abuse in childhood*, Triangle, London, 1991.
Her story, with theological reflections and aids to healing.

Iwaniec, Dorota, *The Emotionally Abused and Neglected Child*, John Wiley and Sons, New York, 1996.
Looks at emotional abuse and neglect and asks whether emotional damage to a child can be repaired. It considers the different types of injury, both active and passive, physical and emotional, that stop children from reaching their full potential.

Kennedy, Margaret, *The Courage to Tell: Christian survivors of sexual abuse tell their stories of pain and hope*, Churches Together in Britain and Ireland, London, 1999.
Powerful stories, challenge to churches and creative worship resources.

Morrison, Jan, *A Safe Place: beyond sexual abuse*, Harold Shaw Publishers, Illinois, 1990.
A book on child sexual abuse and recovery, aimed at teenagers.

Nixson, R., *Home is Where the Hurt is: Domestic Violence and the Church's Response*, Grove Books, Cambridge, 1994.

Parkinson, Patrick, *Child Sexual Abuse and the Churches*, Hodder & Stoughton, London, 1997.
Essential reading for all church leaders and concerned Christians. New edition available.

Pelzer, Dave, *A Child Called It*, Orion, London, 2000.
First of a trilogy describing Dave's horrific childhood and inspiring healing journey.

Richardson, Sue and Bacon, Heather, *Creative Responses to Child Sexual Abuse*, Jessica Kingsley, London, 2001.
Despite heightened media attention and the increase in professional knowledge about child abuse, many children are still being failed by the system. This book outlines ways that the cycle of abuse can be broken.

Wilson, Kate and James, Adrian, *The Child Protection Handbook*, Baillière Tindall, Edinburgh, 2001.
A comprehensive sourcebook and reference for the wide range of practical, theoretical and legal issues in the field of child protection. Practical accounts of the main contemporary developments in child protection practice in the UK.

Wyckoff, Jerry and Unell, Barbara, *Discipline Without Shouting or Spanking*, Meadowbrook Press, Deephaven, MN, 1997.
Provides advice to parents on practical and non-violent solutions for correcting behavioural problems, so as to avoid inadvertent child abuse.

Caring About Abuse, Prevention and Support, various contributors, CCPAS, 2001.
A knowledgeable and practical collection of articles from this specialist charity.

6 Spiritual and pastoral abuse

I have not been able to find any organization working specifically in this area. There are a few agencies whose work touches on this whose details are repeated below.

S:VOX – A voice for abuse survivors and those who support them
(See section 2, p. 157.)

Minister and Clergy Sexual Abuse Survivors (MACSAS)
(See section 2, p. 157.)

The Prevention of Professional Abuse Network (POPAN)
(See section 2, p. 158.)

Cult Information Centre
BCM Cults, London WC1N 3XX.
Tel: 0870 777 3800
Web: <http://www.cultinformation.org.uk>
Information and advice about religious and therapeutic cults.

Published resources

Arterburn, Stephen and Felton, Jack, *Toxic Faith*, Oliver-Nelson, Nashville, TN, 1991.

Beasley-Murray, Peter, *Power for God's Sake: power and abuse in the local church*, Paternoster Press, Carlisle, 1998.
Accessible 'reality-check' of abuse of power and biblical teaching. Practical response.

Blue, Ken, *Healing Spiritual Abuse*, InterVarsity Press, Downers Grove, IL, 1993.
Abusive power in churches, how to escape and avoid it.

Hopkins, Nancy M., *The Congregational Response to Clergy Betrayals of Trust*, Liturgical Press, Collegeville, MN, 1998.

Horst, Elisabeth, *Recovering the Lost Self: Shame-Healing for Victims of Clergy Sexual Abuse*, Liturgical Press, Collegeville, MN, 1998.

Howard, Roland, *The Rise and Fall of the Nine O'Clock Service*, Mowbray, London, 1996.
How abuse of power resulted in emotional, spiritual and sexual abuse within this emerging church.

Johnson, David and VanVonderen, Jeff, *The Subtle Power of Spiritual Abuse*, Bethany House Publishers, Minneapolis, 1991.

Methodist Church, *Report on Sexual Harassment and Abuse*, Methodist Church, 1997.
Mainly about adults.

Ormerod, Neil and Thea, *When Ministers Sin: Sexual Abuse in the Churches*, Millennium Books, Alexandria (Aus.), 1995.

Parsons, Stephen, *Ungodly Fear, Fundamentalist Christianity and the Abuse of Power*, Lion, Oxford, 2000.
Deals with all examples of abuse with a thoughtful, sensitive and practical approach.

Plante, Thomas (ed.), *Bless me Father For I Have Sinned: Perspectives on Sexual Abuse Committed by Roman Catholic Priests*, Praeger, Westport, CT, 1999.

7 Abusers and those at risk of abusing

Parentline Plus
(See section 5, p. 164.)

Stop it Now! UK
PO Box 9841, Birmingham B48 7WB.
Tel: 01527 598184 Helpline 0808 1000 900
Email: <office@stopitnow.org.uk> Web: <http://www.stopitnow.org.uk>
Call the helpline if you are worried about your own thoughts or behaviour
towards children or you suspect that someone you know is sexually
abusing a child, or email: <help@stopitnow.org.uk>
*Stop it Now! UK & Ireland is a major national and local campaign that
aims to stop child sexual abuse by encouraging abusers and potential
abusers to seek help, and by giving adults the information they need to
protect children effectively.*

The Lucy Faithfull Foundation
(See section 5, p. 165.)

Circles of Support and Accountability
The Lucy Faithfull Foundation, PO Box 6740, Chelmsford, Essex
CM2 9WD.
Tel: 01245 265029
Email: <DickFootUK@hotmail.com>
*Project that provides support to sex offenders to reintegrate into the
community and reduce the risk of re-offending. Pilot projects currently
running.*

Everyman Project
Tel: 020 7737 6747
*Counselling, support and advice to men who are violent or concerned
about their violence, and anyone affected by that violence.*

RESPOND
(See section 2, p. 159.)

Published resources
Nolan, Lord, *A Programme for Action: Final Report of the Independent
Review in Child Sexual Protection in the Catholic Church in England and
Wales*, Catholic Bishops' Conference of England and Wales, 2001.
*Covers abuse within the church and dealing with offenders as well as child
protection.*

Appendix 1

Sample child protection reporting procedure

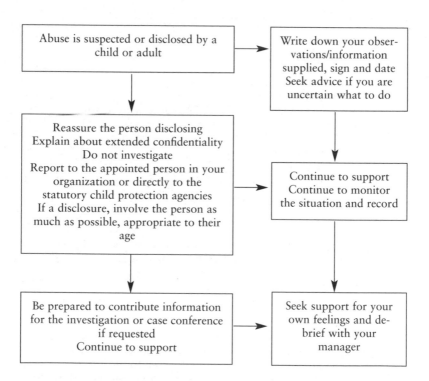

Abuse is suspected or disclosed by a child or adult

→

Write down your observations/information supplied, sign and date
Seek advice if you are uncertain what to do

↓

Reassure the person disclosing
Explain about extended confidentiality
Do not investigate
Report to the appointed person in your organization or directly to the statutory child protection agencies
If a disclosure, involve the person as much as possible, appropriate to their age

→

Continue to support
Continue to monitor the situation and record

↓

Be prepared to contribute information for the investigation or case conference if requested
Continue to support

→

Seek support for your own feelings and de-brief with your manager

Key guidelines for responding to a disclosure:

- Accept what the person says.
- Explain about extended confidentiality.
- Do not push for information or question a victim of abuse.
- Be honest and remain calm.
- Reassure the person you are glad they told you, it is not the victim's fault, you are taking this very seriously.
- Reassure the person you have listened, understood and will act to help them, involving them as far as possible.
- Be aware the young person may have been threatened or intimidated.

Appendix 2

You have reported suspected abuse – what happens next?

---◄O►---

Stage	Notes
Referral received	You will be asked the nature of your concerns, how and why they have arisen, what they are based on and whether the child may need urgent action to make them safe.
Decision on next course of action – should happen within 24 hours	Discussion with referrer and other relevant agencies (parents' permission needed to discuss with third parties unless it may put child at risk). Discussion about whether there are concerns about child's health or development or available evidence on actual or potential harm which justifies further enquiries, assessment and/or intervention. Social Services may decide: • no further action • no risk but child and family require services to meet needs that are affecting child's welfare • child may be at risk and further assessment needed This may be coupled with emergency intervention if immediate risk to the child is likely and involvement of the police if a crime is suspected
Initial assessment – should happen within seven working days	Social Services gather information and make an assessment using the *Framework for Assessment*. The child, family (if safe) and other agencies involved with the child (e.g. churches) are contacted for information. The aim is to ascertain if there is a reasonable cause to suspect the child is suffering, or likely to suffer, significant harm. A decision is made as to whether action is required to safeguard and promote the child's welfare. The initial assessment period may be very brief if the child may be in immediate risk of harm, in which case an Emergency Protection Order may be sought from the Courts.

Stage	Notes
Strategy Discussion	When there is reasonable cause to suspect significant harm, a strategy discussion must be held, involving Social Services, the police and other appropriate agencies (e.g. school, referring agency, health workers, youth workers).
	The purpose is for all agencies to act together – share information, plan the process, discuss info sharing with the family and who does what to support the child.
	The meeting may conclude that: • no further action is necessary *or* • the issue is one of need rather than risk *or* • there is enough evidence of risk for a 'Section 47 Enquiry' to take place . . . planning for this discussed • emergency action is needed
Section 47 Enquiry – to be completed within 37 working days	A 'Core Assessment' is conducted using the *Framework for Assessment* to collect and analyse information. The assessment may encompass siblings or other children.
	Investigative interviews with the Police may take place for criminal proceedings. Any interviews with the child should be conducted by specialists. The child may refuse to participate.
	The outcome of the enquiry may be: • concerns are not substantiated • concerns are substantiated but the child is not judged to be at continuing risk of significant harm • concerns are substantiated and the child is judged to be at continuing risk of significant harm. In this case, the next stage of the procedure is implemented – the Initial Child Protection Conference

Appendix 3

Developing good practice in child protection

————◦————

(The headings are taken from the government guidelines *Safe from Harm*, HMSO, 1999)

1 ADOPT A POLICY STATEMENT ON SAFEGUARDING THE WELFARE OF CHILDREN
   • Make sure everyone knows the policy and procedures

2 PLAN THE WORK OF THE ORGANIZATION SO AS TO MINIMIZE SITUATIONS WHERE THE ABUSE OF CHILDREN MAY OCCUR
   • Have enough leaders for each age group
   • Never work alone or behind closed doors
   • Avoid transporting children alone and use back seat and seatbelts
   • Remember leader–child relationship boundaries
   • Keep touch safe
   • Always seek appropriate parental consent
   • Keep relevant medical information and emergency contacts
   • Have a first-aid kit and get trained
   • Record injuries and accidents and tell parents
   • Check premises for health and safety
   • Be properly insured

3 INTRODUCE A SYSTEM WHEREBY CHILDREN MAY TALK WITH AN INDEPENDENT PERSON
   • Listen to children
   • Ensure appropriate training
   • Tell the children about your system

4 APPLY AGREED PROCEDURES FOR PROTECTING CHILDREN TO ALL PAID STAFF AND VOLUNTEERS

5 GIVE ALL PAID STAFF AND VOLUNTEERS CLEAR ROLES

6 USE SUPERVISION AS A MEANS OF PROTECTING CHILDREN
   - Always supervise visitors and unvetted helpers
   - Support leaders and avoid isolation and overload
   - Share concerns about colleagues
   - Work as a team

7 TREAT ALL WOULD-BE PAID STAFF AND VOLUNTEERS AS JOB APPLICANTS FOR ANY POSITION INVOLVING CONTACT WITH CHILDREN
   - Use job descriptions, appointment procedures and volunteer contracts

8 GAIN AT LEAST ONE REFERENCE FROM A PERSON WHO HAS EXPERIENCE OF THE APPLICANTS' PAID WORK OR VOLUNTEERING WITH CHILDREN

9 EXPLORE ALL APPLICANTS' EXPERIENCE OF WORKING OR CONTACT WITH CHILDREN IN AN INTERVIEW BEFORE APPOINTMENT

10 FIND OUT WHETHER AN APPLICANT HAS ANY CONVICTION FOR CRIMINAL OFFENCES AGAINST CHILDREN
   - Vet all leaders through the new Criminal Records Bureau

11 MAKE PAID AND VOLUNTARY APPOINTMENTS CONDITIONAL ON THE SUCCESSFUL COMPLETION OF A PROBATIONARY PERIOD

12 ISSUE GUIDELINES ON HOW TO DEAL WITH THE DISCLOSURE OR DISCOVERY OF ABUSE
   - Tell parents about your policy and practice

13 TRAIN PAID STAFF AND VOLUNTEERS, THEIR LINE MANAGERS OR SUPERVISORS, AND POLICY MAKERS IN THE PREVENTION OF CHILD ABUSE
   - Use recommended training agencies
   - Ensure all with contact with children are trained and updated regularly

Appendix 4

Sample reporting procedure for adults

——◄○►——

This is an example of an approach that could be adapted appropriately to the organization, with reference to other relevant policies such as the complaints procedure and code of practice.

1 An adult makes a complaint of abuse by someone in a position of trust within the organization. (This disclosure may be made to any member of the organization.)

2 The disclosure is referred to an independent listener or complaints officer, whose role is to support the person making the complaint, listen carefully to what they have to say and decide the next course of action, according to the level of severity of the complaint, the role of the person against whom the complaint has been made and the wishes of the person making the complaint.

3 There are several possible courses of action, which should be taken by the independent listener and the complainant working together:
  (a) The independent listener supports the complainant to take the issue to the supervisor or management group immediately responsible for the person against whom the complaint has been made. Investigation, discussion and possible resolution of the complaint may then follow standard grievance and disciplinary procedures.
  (b) In more serious cases, or where the immediate management group is implicated in the complaint or unable to resolve it, an independent complaints process involving senior managers and an independent expert consultant should deal with the issue.
  (c) In the most serious cases, or where the complaint is against a more senior person, the complaint should be referred directly to a more senior level; for example, a regional leader or national officer. In the case of independent groups that have no wider affiliation, an outside organization with relevant expertise should be involved in assisting with the investigation.

4 There are key principles which should be followed whichever course of action is chosen:

(a) Pastoral support should be provided for both the person disclosing the abuse and the person against whom the complaint is being made.

(b) This support should be independent of the investigation process and should not be the same person for both parties.

(c) The investigation and attempts at resolution should ideally be undertaken with the involvement of an independent expert who can assist in interpretation of the information available, ensuring fairness and an open process that all can trust, and advise as to the appropriate course of action.

(d) Investigation should not normally include a confrontation between the victim and their abuser. This is potentially abusive and unlikely to assist in discovering the truth.

(e) Staff whose role may include dealing with disclosures of abuse in any capacity, including those with management/leadership responsibilities, pastoral supporters and the independent listener/complaints officer, should receive appropriate training.

5 A code of conduct that makes it clear what is appropriate behaviour and boundaries for people in positions of trust and what is abusive behaviour, provides a key foundation for the processes of investigation and resolution.

6 A disciplinary and grievance procedure should describe the normal course of action for different levels and categories of inappropriate behaviour.

7 Because a position of trust is built on relationship and is not merely a functional role, the normal outcomes of a disciplinary procedure are unlikely to be the end of the issue. The effects on the person who has made the disclosure are not addressed simply by giving someone a written warning, for example. The principle of restitution and the goal of reconciliation should form the basis of a process of resolution after the complaints and disciplinary procedures have been completed.

(a) Recommendations may have been made as part of these procedures, which can assist resolution of the issue. This may take some considerable time, and may involve further action months or even years after the first stages of dealing with the issue.

(b) Both primary and secondary victims may need support and counselling to aid their healing. Restitution could include the organization or the abuser paying for this support.

(c) The abuser may need counselling and training to understand and modify their behaviour.

(d) The organization may need to review and change practices that could have contributed to the abuse taking place.

(e) The independent listener could explore with the victim what else would assist restoration. This may include a meeting with the person who abused them, with appropriate assistance. All parties have to be prepared for such a reconciliation process and willing to engage; this state may not be reached for some time, if at all.

8 Where a direct reconciliation is not possible or appropriate, other means may be used to assist all parties involved to achieve closure. For example, a written apology from the perpetrator or the organization, a service of acknowledgement and healing, a creative process of confession and absolution.

9 These procedures should adopt an inquisitorial rather than adversarial approach. All perspectives should be considered when deciding on an appropriate course of action, but care should be taken not to place the needs of the organization or the alleged abuser above those of the victim.

10 The voice of the victim has too often been silenced by the abuse and responses to it. In developing and implementing procedures like these, organizations should involve and consult people with relevant experience and knowledge of abuse, including survivors.

Appendix 5

Positive pampering

————◄○►————

Here are 15 ideas for methods that can help survivors to deal with their issues and suffering, moving away from strategies that are harmful to self or others. The first few ideas are immediate strategies to replace self-harming behaviour. The rest are a range of ways to support the healing journey. Most of these are tried and tested by many different people. Not everything will work for everybody; try those that appeal and use them to inspire you to find your own.

1 If you feel you need to self-harm, try to identify a safer alternative action that mimics your normal method. For example, instead of cutting, draw on your arm with red pen, wear an elastic band and 'ping' it to give a slight sting.

2 If you are trying to overcome an eating disorder, try methods that help you to remain in control and feel more positive about food and your body. For example, arrange to eat on your own if you are uncomfortable in public; eat larger portions of healthy low-carbohydrate foods like vegetables and fruit, lean meat or soya meat-replacement; then treat yourself to small portions of special foods like ice-cream or chocolate as a reward.

3 Express strong emotions rather than suppressing or hiding them, but in safe ways. If possible, find a friend to try these ideas with you. Try smashing old china, cutting or tearing up newspaper or pulverizing cardboard boxes. Throw stones into a river or the sea. Go to a wild and private place like the top of a hill, the middle of a field or wood, and shout and scream as loud as you can. Watch a sad film and have a really good cry. Draw or paint your feelings on big sheets of paper. Model with plasticine or clay. Whack a cushion with a tennis racket or another cushion. Kick a ball or hit a punchbag. Dance wildly to some loud music. Make a big pile of autumn leaves then mess it all up. In summer, have a water-fight or mud-fight!

4 If you are trying to give up self-harming habits of any kind, give yourself a reward for each goal you achieve. Take one day at a time to start with, then it's not so far back to the beginning if you have a little lapse. Try buying a pack of fun stickers and mark a calendar or chart each day;

then add rewards for each week, month and year! Reward yourself with positive treats – not alcohol, cigarettes, etc. Try budget retail therapy – only charity shops and discount stores are allowed; set a budget, e.g. 99p for small items, under £5 for clothes. Find something that makes you feel really good, like a special-occasion top, or that you can enjoy, like a book or hobby item.

5 Read the psalms out loud. They are full of passion and strong negative and positive emotions. If you can't pray but want to communicate with God, they provide a great way to do so!

6 Write poetry, read it aloud to yourself or a trusted friend. Several survivors' websites publish poetry on-line too.

7 Write or draw your own story. You may never want to show it to anyone else, but it least it has been laid out. Keep a journal of your healing journey too; noting feelings, events, things you are struggling with, celebrations, what has helped you. Later you can look back and see your progress.

8 Build a friendship with another survivor. If you don't know any you can make contact through survivors' sites on the web, or a survivors' group. It is so good to know you are not the only one and that a lot of your experiences are similar. You can support and encourage each other. You can talk about your feelings and issues with someone who needs fewer explanations, and share the burden beyond your immediate family and friends.

9 Practise loving and caring for yourself better. Pamper your body a little. Have a relaxing bath or shower with nice smellies, and then rub in some moisturizer or oil. If you find this difficult, start somewhere small like your hands or knees. Look at them carefully while you are massaging and respect the parts of your life they bear witness to. Practise touching them tenderly, enjoying and appreciating your body and taking good care of it. If you don't find it triggering, booking a professional massage or getting a friend or partner to give you one is very relaxing.

10 Especially if you were abused as a child, there may be childhood experiences you missed out on or couldn't enjoy. All of us can benefit from giving our inner child a treat! Go to a beach and dig sandcastles, swing in the park, blow bubbles, take your teddy bear on a picnic, read a children's book, make plasticine models.

11 Teddy bears are great companions. You can tell them everything that you may find it hard to tell friends and counsellors. You can get angry with them, cry with them, cuddle them, throw them – and they will never abandon or abuse you. If you live on your own, they provide something to cuddle in bed and to talk to in the night. You can get little ones that fit on a key-ring or in a pocket when you're out.

12 Once a month at least, do something you enjoy and that brings you pleasure and takes you away from the abuse. Go dancing, watch a film, play, ballet, opera, visit a museum or garden, play at a theme park, take a boat ride, go to the zoo.

13 If church and prayer are difficult, but you want to keep your relationship with God, try more creative ways to do so. Some alternative worship groups run informal and inclusive services and gatherings that are much easier for survivors. The natural world is the best setting for prayer and worship; it can be instinctive to praise and talk with God walking by a river, in a bluebell wood, at the top of a hill, in a garden humming with insects and birds.

14 Create your own liturgy to express your healing journey; actions and symbols to express anger, pain, mourning, struggle, growth, achievement, new life, restoration. Write prayers you can't say aloud and burn them. Light candles in support of other survivors. Make a pile of stones in memory of those who didn't survive, and the burden on victims. Plant bulbs to symbolize new life.

15 Keep believing that you are loved and valued and worth as much as every other human being that God created. Tell yourself this every day, recording over the bad messages from the abuser that you might have in your head. Be your own best friend; take care of your needs, practise giving and receiving love, find help when things are hard. Find little ways to encourage and support yourself. Write yourself little notes, put post-its round the house where you will discover them, take your teddy on a difficult trip, buy a bunch of flowers, wrap up a chocolate bar as a present.

Appendix 6

Direct work with survivors

————◇————

Many individuals and agencies may be offering a variety of services to survivors; in both one-to-one and group-work contexts. Certain approaches have demonstrated their worth in different settings, and a common core of good practice guidelines has emerged:

1 Believe the victim
Be a patient and gentle listener, encouraging victims to reveal their own story in their own time and at their own depth. Reassure that telling and taking action are good things, however scary and painful. Be consistently there (within whatever boundaries of time and involvement are realistic).

2 Survivors are experts in their own healing
Let people keep responsibility for their lives and the key decisions they need to make. Avoid the temptation to rescue or provide your solutions. Recognize the fear, pain and need to find endurance and trust that are characteristic of the early stages of the healing journey.

3 Work with survivors at their own pace
Don't rush the telling or the response. Encourage safety of self and any family, provide information and support, including a safe space to release the strong emotions of hurt and anger. Walk alongside, accompanying the key steps if possible – this is good support. But leave the control with the survivor.

4 Place the responsibility for the abuse firmly on the shoulders of the abusers
All abuse survivors have some feelings of guilt and shame and responsibility for what has happened; it is part of the nature of abuse. Be a constant reminder that no one deserves to be treated like that and that the blame is the perpetrator's alone.

5 Put abuse in the context of power relations
Be clear yourself and with the victim that it was the imbalance of power between them and the abuser that sustained the abuse and meant they were probably powerless to stop it. Many victims beat themselves up for 'allowing it to happen'. Reinforce the responsibility of authority/leadership not to take advantage of the vulnerable in their care.[1]

Note

1 Adapted from Whelan, Anna, 'Working Space, Youth Work and Sexual Abuse Survivors', *Youth and Policy*, No. 46, 1994.

Index